Going to the Well

A Mother–Daughter Journey

Additional Reviews

This is a mother-daughter story unlike any other. Based on actual taped sessions, the book details how the author and her mother move from estrangement to individual self-discovery. Ultimately, they experience appreciation and mutual respect. Packed with empathy and pathos, rage and resentment, understanding and forgiveness, *Going to the Well* is a page-turner that brings to life the harsh realities of rural living in the American Midwest of the early 1900s. Underlying the storyline is an inspiring search for self, sanity and true spiritual identity.

—**Jeanette Keil**, author of *Invitation to Wellness*

Going to the Well offers a wonderful read and deep insights. Roeder's memoir presents an extensive family history that is both unique and strangely universal. The individuals and the events described belong exclusively to her family's long history, but they indirectly reflect the trials and triumphs of our own families. This book prompts all of its readers to look into the events in our own lives that make us who we are. I could not help wishing that I could have had my mother or father on tape telling me the details of our family's struggles and successes.

—**John Fink, Ph.D.**, English, Ball State University

Going to the Well

A Mother-Daughter Journey

Nancy Key Roeder

ISBN: 978-1-935514-16-9
Library of Congress Control Number: 2011930988

Cover art: Ron Sumners
Cover design by Pam Knight

Plain View Press
P.O. 42255
Austin, TX 78704

plainviewpress.net
pk@plainviewpress.net
512-441-2452

This book is dedicated to

Joe and Dave,

both treasured memories

Acknowledgements

Grateful acknowledgment for permission to reprint copyrighted material from the following authors and/or publications: "The Path" in *Still Breathing* by Antoinette Roeder, Berkeley: Apocryphile Press, 2010; *Womenfolks: Growing Up Down South* by Shirley Abbott, Boston: Houghton Mifflin, 1983, (quote heading Chapter 2); *Through the Garden Gate* edited by Bill Neal, Chapel Hill, NC: University of North Carolina Press, 1990, in a reprinted essay by Elizabeth Lawrence, "Gardens of Childhood," which first appeared in 1960 in *The Charlotte Observer*, Charlotte, North Carolina,(quote heading Chapter 5); *The Power of Now: A Guide to Spiritual Enlightenment* by Eckhart Tolle, New World Library, Novato, California and Namaste Publishing, Vancouver, B.C., Canada, 1999, (quote heading Chapter 13); Pierre Teilhard de Chardin. BrainyQuote.com, Xplore Inc. 2010 (http://www.brainyquote.com/quotes/quotes/p/pierretell160888.html), (quote heading Chapter 15).

Every effort has been made to secure permissions for material quoted in this book. All quotations have been credited. Any additional copyright holders are invited to contact the author so that proper credit can be given in future editions.

With Gratitude

Many people contributed to the creation of this book. My gratitude is profound.

Robert Latham, dear friend and minister, saw merit in the transforming relationship between mother and daughter and felt that the journey of the two women resonated also with men as a universal experience. Thanks also to his wife Cindy Latham, who offered valuable marketing ideas and strategies.

Antoinette Roeder, my sister-in-law and published poet, granted use of her poem in the Introduction and generously spent time reading portions of the manuscript as it evolved. Her husband Michael Roeder, my brother-in-law and photographer *par excellence*, assisted me in understanding some of the technicalities around old photos.

I am grateful also to Marsha Willis, daughter of my late husband Joe Willis. I respect her judgment as a successful author and appreciate her candid comments and suggestions for strengthening the language. Marsha's husband Mark Lawson, a voracious reader and discerning critic of all forms of writing, expressed keen observations of my mother's character as depicted in the story and found the manuscript a worthy read.

Numerous friends have read the manuscript and offered valuable critiques. Jeanette Keil, long-time friend from a writing group in San Diego in the 1970s, suggested ways to improve wording and transitions. Barbara Bailey, Barbara Merchant, Irene Spahr, Sally Ganster, Susie Streng, Judy Miller, Adella Schulz, and Donna and Mark Stavig shared optimistic and encouraging remarks. Jane Lawless and Stephanie Briggs, eagle-eyed editors and proofreaders, caught typos and contributed constructive ideas. Amanda Bloom and Lorie Dwinell, both veterans of the publishing world, provided valuable information and supportive comments. Jack Fink, a co-author with me on another book, responded favorably as a male reader to the unfolding relationship of mother and daughter and to the shared dialogues on religious beliefs. Marci Mustoe, a mental health professional, and Mary Hamilton, a retired school counselor, grasped well my mother's struggle to choose the path leading toward mental health. I could not have been blessed with better friendships.

The support of my family cannot be overestimated. My husband Dave Roeder, who unfortunately passed away just prior to publication, patiently endured reading through many versions and put forth beneficial suggestions. My daughter Julie Holmes helped me with matters technological. My sister Shari Brooks provided old family photos, which I thought had gone astray. To crosscheck my mother's memory of some of the details of family history, I relied on materials created for our cousins' reunion of 1992: a family history written by my cousin Joe Parriott and a genealogy prepared by another cousin, Joe Downey. To all of you, for your help and understanding, I am deeply grateful.

Kudos go to Pam Knight for taking the reins of Plain View Press after the tragic death of the publisher, Susan Bright, who had accepted this book for publication. Pam and her able assistants guided the manuscript through the publication process with great efficiency.

Seeds for this book were sown in long conversations with my now deceased cousin, Karen Danley, a director at the Center for Psychiatric Rehabilitation located on the campus of Boston University, who urged me to write about our grandmother's tragedy instead of hiding it and who located the hospital records, excerpts of which appear in Chapter 7. Finally, I would be remiss if I failed to mention the legacies of two other people who played roles in bringing forth this book: my late husband Joe Willis, an author himself, whose deep scholarly understanding of the Bible influenced my religious perspective shared with my mother in Chapters 14 and 15; and most of all, my mother, without whose guiding spirit and willingness to let me record her story, this book never would have been written.

Author's Note

My mother's story is based on twenty-two taped interviews spanning sixteen years between 1977 and 1993. We began the project on the pretext of preserving her memories of growing up on a farm in rural America in the early part of the twentieth century. But I also had another motive: to approach her in some way that might lead to the healing of past mother-daughter wounds, for at the time we were emotionally estranged. As I learned the difficulty of the life she led, I joined her on the path of understanding and gained insight into the causes of our early mother-daughter conflicts. I became filled with admiration for her decisions, which brought her from despair to hope. Over these several years, we managed to reconcile the hurts that harbored in our hearts. I celebrate the power of intergenerational storytelling as the vehicle that helped us reach a place of rapport and reconciliation.

Memory is fallible, and emotional memory will vary from person to person. Living descendants who recognize some of the family history recorded herein might respond, "But I heard it differently." Their understandings, passed along from my mother's siblings, might not correspond with the personal, candid revelations of a woman never entirely understood by the family in which she grew up. Yet, they stand as authentically experienced, with as much "truth" as anyone else's perceptions.

Two voices emerge in this double-vision memoir. My words contain reflections, explanations and memories triggered by our conversations. For the most part, my mother's voice carries the story of her own life. To the extent possible, I have preserved this voice, with its conversational expressions and occasional flares of emotion. However, this is not a verbatim report. I have selected some stories but not all, and I have added material from off-tape conversations and from letters she wrote. I have condensed the content, which over the years repeated and recycled itself. To shield the identities of living descendants, I have created fictitious names of family members and most (but not all) geographical regions and places. The family photos are authentic, but the captions bear the pseudonyms as chosen for the characters.

As I began to weave this book together, I saw a pattern emerging. Here was the time-honored tale of a spiritual odyssey, not limited to any particular religious faith. I began to see my mother's life lived out with mythic elements, moving through stages of truth telling (revelations) to insight (redemption) to wisdom (transformation). She fought psychological dragons and descended often into despair, but she also reached deeply into her soul to tap a wellspring of inner strength. The journey extended over her long lifetime. Central to her quest was the search for a God of harmony, love and peace. But first, she had to discard a punitive deity. And she had to forgive. In the last years of her life, she was serene in the knowledge that she had found a God with whom she could be in relationship. As we moved through the years of tape recording her stories, I gradually released a perception of my mother as mythic witch and began to see her transformed into that of human heroine.

This interpretation of my mother's life as the universal mythic journey is strictly my own, and it comes from viewing her story through new lenses.

Contents

Acknowledgements   6
With Gratitude   7
Author's Note   9
Introduction   15
The Path   15

Prologue: Alpha and Omega   **21**

Endings: November 2002   23
Beginnings: September 1977   27

Part One—Revelation   **31**

Chapter 1: Madness   33
Chapter 2: Family Tree   41
Chapter 3: Family Prayer   57
Chapter 4: "The Short and Simple Annals of the Poor"   67
Chapter 5: In the Garden: Memories Caught   79
Chapter 6: Innocence Lost   95
Chapter 7: After the Madness: Masks   103
Chapter 8: Madness Returned: Emma   121

Part Two—Redemption   **135**

Chapter 9: How an Angel Got Her Wings   137
Chapter 10: Memorabilia   151
Chapter 11: Loves, Losses, Luck   159
Chapter 12: Reflections on Redemption   171

Part Three—Transformation   **175**

Chapter 13: Born Again   177
Chapter 14: A Dialogue on Faith: Beginning   187
Chapter 15: A Dialogue on Faith: Continuing   201
Afterword   217
Chapter 16: Lessons from the Well: A Daughter's
             Redemption   219

Epilogue: November 2003   225
Appendix: Some Writings
From Emma's "Bits and Pieces"   227
Two Poems by Laura Catherine Delaney Johnson   228

Discussion Questions   231
About the Author   233

Memory is the mother of all wisdom.

—Samuel Johnson

Introduction

The Path

When you have followed the map
which is not a map

and created the path with every
step

You will traverse the in-ferno
meet the dragons and find them
tame.

You will bathe in
the pool of the past and empty it.

You will cross the desert and fall in love with life teeming there

and you will emerge where
the luminous world swoons at your
feet, seeking what only you
can give.

Antoinette Voûte Roeder
From *Still Breathing*, 2010
Apocryphile Press, Berkeley, CA

This is the story of an unknown heroine's spiritual journey from darkness to light. She was not famous, not royal, not rich. The journey was not pre-determined, nor was it linear. It had its growth spurts and setbacks. But in the end, this tale recounts her struggle to understand the truth of her life and her growth toward spiritual and mental health.

Unlike the male heroes of mythology and literature, this particular heroine embarked upon her quest unconsciously, without defined goals. She did not set out in some flamboyant way to seek the Holy Grail. She did not plan it this way, but hers was a mythic journey that led from the revelation of family tragedies to redemption through forgiveness, and finally to transformation of her soul. As any knight-errant, along the way, she battled inner dragons and subdued them, only to find others standing in her way. With trepidation, she inched her way rung by rung until she emerged out of dread and fear into confidence and hope.

She was my mother, an ordinary—yet extraordinary—woman who grew up in rural America in the early part of the twentieth century. Part of this story arises from the era in which she lived. But time and place, while important, do not drive its essential core. Rather they form a backdrop, like a stage set, on which the journey is acted out in mythic ways. It is commonplace—and a mistake—to view that bygone world through a single lens: a simple world unburdened by material abundance and media overload, a quaint era filled with happy, loving families with only minor stresses, a safe place removed from child predators.

Think instead of a child's kaleidoscope. Upon first peering down the tube, one can see gem-like colored pieces falling chaotically before one's eye. As the tube is turned, the multiple mirrors forming the prism collect the free-fall into an infinite number of visual patterns. Thus, my mother's story achieves coherence through a complex understanding of the sociological and psychological dimensions of common family struggles in any age or culture—of survival and denial, shame and recrimination, forgiveness and redemption.

Born in 1899 and raised on an isolated farm near the Ohio Valley, my mother began teaching in a rural school and later gained admittance to a nursing program at an Ivy League university. A year after graduation, she moved west where she met and married my father in Arizona. When I was three, they moved to New Mexico where I grew up. Later, my mother and father re-located to California for a brief few years. Ultimately, they returned to New Mexico. The taped interviews began in San Diego and ended in Albuquerque. Shortly after our last taping session in 1993, she fell and broke her arm, setting in motion the events that would end our project and necessitate a move closer to where I lived. She died in 2002 at age 103 in Colorado, where she had lived for nine years in an assisted living facility.

How did I learn the details of my mother's journey? Surely not easily, since at one time we were close to becoming estranged. Once I had left home after marrying, I moved around a great deal, and we gradually grew apart both geographically and emotionally. The fault was my own, for I had allowed lingering resentments—those unresolved feelings of anger left over from childhood—to fester, to poison my heart.

Our mother-daughter wars arose from our personalities, not from some evil set of unjust punishments. She was the quiet perfectionist; I was the gregarious pragmatist. We both were dreamers of different sorts but did not realize how much we shared that trait until our reconciliation years later.

Could the tape project be the path to healing our rift? When I proposed doing the interviews, my mother responded eagerly by sharing a treasure trove of memories. I responded warmly and expressed my appreciation for all that she had revealed to me. Together, we moved over time to bridge what once might have been an irreparable chasm of separation.

When I play the tapes, I think of that day in November when she left this world. Her date of death fell close to the day she had given birth to me over sixty years before. I hear my mother's voice, the voice that told the truth. But I hear myself also, and I realize that we have grown closer, have pardoned each other our imperfections and have redeemed a relationship gone awry.

This story is not hers alone. Nor is it exclusively mine or ours together. It is also that of all the ordinary but very extraordinary women in the world, who think they do not matter, who believe that they do not have voices. It is the remarkable journey of facing the truth of one's own life in unspoken and unassuming ways. It is about strife and courage, tragedy and triumph. But another element imposes itself. Through the sharing of stories can come the healing of mother-daughter estrangement, along with arrival together in a place of hope and inner peace.

Prologue: Alpha and Omega

The Bustle in a House
The Morning after Death
Is solemnest of industries
Enacted up Earth –

The Sweeping up the Heart
And putting Love away
We shall not want to use again
Until Eternity.
                —Emily Dickinson, Poem 1078

The very tones in which we spake
Had something strange, I could but mark;
The leaves of memory seemed to make
A mournful rustling in the dark.

                One stanza of "The Fire of Drift-Wood"
                —Henry Wadsworth Longfellow

Endings

November 2002

My cell phone rang the moment I clicked my remote to open the car door. Somehow, I knew it would be the nurse at the long-term care facility. But I was shocked to hear her say that I needed to come immediately because my mother was dying. Last week, a cold; this week, pneumonia; and now, the end time.

Backing the car out of the garage, I heard a crunch. The rear view mirror on the right side had caught the side of the garage and snapped back, nearly tearing away from my Subaru station wagon. Lucky that time, I thought. I forced myself to crawl through the winding street in our tucked-away neighborhood. But once I reached the boulevard, I began speeding with abandon, glancing all the while for the expected flashing red light of a police car. My mind was gripped with one goal: to deliver my lesson plans to the high school where I had begun teaching part-time and then race to the nursing home with all deliberate speed. No cops today. My addled brain uttered nonsensically, "Thank you."

Alighting from my car, I got blasted by a chunk of chilly Rocky Mountain air. It smacked me awake, alerting a brain already dissolving into a surreal fog. The cold sliced at my exposed fingers—in the rush of leaving the house, I had forgotten my gloves. I began to run from the school parking lot to the main building. It was frigid but brilliantly sunny, and warm rays poured themselves into ever-moving golden puddles at my feet, glinting as if real water formed on the dry black asphalt. Fortunately, students were already in class, so my chaotic journey probably went unobserved. I dodged between cars with impunity, cutting the distance—the equivalent of a city block—by at least a third.

Once inside, I bolted through hallways and corridors and barged into the main office, oblivious to startled secretaries, students and counselors. Dumping my notebooks and briefcases on the head secretary's desk, I croaked, "You'll have to get a substitute—I'm needed at the nursing home. My mother is near death."

"But wait!" came an unanswered plea from the astonished secretary.

With no further explanation, I turned, reversed my frantic course back through the throngs of students who were changing classes, pushed open the double doors leading to the parking lot and fled.

Fifteen minutes later, I was speaking with the nursing staff at Sunnyside Manor. "She didn't wake this morning. We thought ... you know, the antibiotics you approved really did no good. This type of pneumonia is hard on older people. And your mother is over 100 years old," the head nurse told me. Her words were business-like, yet she glanced at me sympathetically. Clearly, she was used to breaking bad news to families.

Trying to calm myself from my frenetic journey, I took a deep breath and entered my mother's room. Her peaceful countenance flooded my agitated soul. Her eyes were closed, and I assumed that by this time she was unconscious. Her breathing was shallow but not labored. The staff had administered, if not the love and nurture she craved all her life, at least those palliative medicines that ease the transition from this life to whatever lies beyond. Her white curls neatly framed a nearly unwrinkled 103-year-old face. Only a few days ago, she had enjoyed her weekly hairdo at the nursing home beauty salon. But today was leave-taking time. She looked calm, pale and remarkably lovely.

One of the nurses approached me in the room. "Why don't you take a break and call anyone you might like. You might need some support. This kind of thing could last for an hour or more." Her tone was gentle, understanding. She knew that my husband had died one month before and that I was about to face the loss of yet another close family member.

I withdrew to a small waiting room, settled in a chair and used my cell phone to call a couple of friends from my church. One of them said that she would come immediately. I walked back to be with my mother, although she had no way of knowing that I was there. I spent those last few moments of her life stroking her forehead, out of some deep buried memory of a similar soothing offered gently and consistently through years to assuage the hurts and bumps of my growing up. By the time Karen arrived, my mother had slipped away.

Be grateful, my logical mind told me. Her passing was easy. There was no struggle, no pain, no regrets. And so to work. Call the mortuary. Thank the staff. Arrange to remove her clothes from the tiny room. Collect the forms signed by the nursing home physician. She had rehearsed with me what to do, my methodical, logical mother. I waited until a mortician arrived from Crown Valley Memorial Park, then walked with him alongside the rolling cart carrying my mother's body.

As we headed down the hall, one of the physical therapists stopped me. "I wanted you to know how much I appreciated your mother. She was so frail these last few weeks, but she was always cheerful. And she tried so hard to make it to the end of the hall, even when it was hard for her. But she was so sweet. I wanted you to know that." It was all I could do to exit the building before giving way to the first wave of grief as the full measure of my loss flooded over me.

My mother died on a brisk November morning before I had a chance to say goodbye. On the way to my car, I stepped on a pile of dry leaves. As if on cue, they formed into a small dust devil, crackled and broke into tiny pieces and swirled upwards, like so many scattered portions of our lives.

Beginnings

September 1977

We began the interviews in California. I had been seeing a psychiatrist for symptoms of depression. Anti-depressants were yet to enter the market in the way that we know them now. Medicines were prescribed only for extreme cases of psychosis. For situational depression, long-term psychotherapy was the *modus operandi*.

"I want to talk about my marriage," I told Dr. Johnson. She steered me away, however, from that topic and asked me to focus on memories of my childhood. I did this with some discomfort and a suspicion that she was trying to drag out our sessions. I know now that I was fortunate to have insurance coverage to provide long-term therapy. The sessions continued for nearly two years.

We eventually got to the marital problems, but meanwhile she probed into tender and hidden recesses of my psyche, lanced boils here and there and brought forth—purposely, I am certain—hot liquid that swept down my cheeks, washing away the detritus of long-hidden pain. While a complete litany of perceived hurts is unnecessary, a few memories linger.

I had trouble with my mother's bossiness, her effort to micro-manage every phase of my life. Mother was a perfectionist, so naturally, I constantly failed to meet her expectations. As a consequence, she judged herself a failure, and we became continually enmeshed in a vicious circle of recrimination, both spoken and unspoken.

I resented the restrictions she imposed, which segregated me from my friends. I was denied permission to go horseback riding because once she had fallen from a horse and sustained a concussion. I could not go tobogganing in the mountains with my church group because I might fall and injure my spine. There were food obsessions and non-existent "allergies" foisted on me that I learned later to discard.

I absorbed these dictums early on and accepted them. Because I was the compliant sort, I did not rebel or act out but rather became increasingly anxious and sad. No child grows up without boundaries, and these were not the things that should have caused such long-term distress. Yet, here I was, in Dr. J.'s office, sobbing over things I thought I had long forgotten.

Often my mother and father would whisper behind my back, as if in collusion. My self-confidence plummeted as these all-powerful people aligned their psychological weapons against me. I should note that my father, who specialized in concocting any number of get-rich-quick schemes, often absented himself from our lives. When he was home, he paid little attention to my needs. He did not disagree with my mother's ways of rearing me, but neither did he collaborate. In short, he acquiesced by choice and became distant from my life. His plans for riches failed to materialize, and we spent years scraping the economic bottom in order to survive. But the story of my father is for another day.

Still, I know that my mother loved me. She read to me from times before I can remember. She went out of her way to introduce me to the beauties of art, literature, poetry and classical music. When I missed the first two months of my ninth grade because of mononucleosis, she sat with me patiently as I conjugated Latin verbs and struggled to understand algebra. She came to all of my school performances and took pride in my scholastic and extra-curricular accomplishments. She encouraged me to find a social group in high school and worked with me to plan parties at our home. When I starred in the senior play, she was there, without my father, who believed that participation in drama was evil. She attended my high school graduation ceremony alone because my father found it important to be somewhere else that night. But the exacting expectations continued unabated—right down to the precise place to set the dishcloth or else endure the shame of being judged a total failure. By the time I reached adulthood, I felt pulled in two directions, juggling polar opposite feelings of intense loyalty along with deep aversion.

For too many years, I buried the negative feelings, believing that I had done something wrong. I had developed my defenses over the years: changing myself to please this other person who exerted so much power over my psychological well-being. In doing so, I bargained that I would not be emotionally punished, and so convinced myself that I had attained happiness, however shallow. Living this dynamic, too young to know myself, I unwisely chose my first husband.

As our therapy sessions continued over the months, Dr. J urged me to confront my mother with my anger and tell her why I had not sought to resume our relationship except on the most superficial basis. Fear struck me. I simply could not do that, I told her. My mother would be hurt and possibly angry, I said, and I simply could not face that prospect. Clearly, the love-hate dynamic still pulled my psyche apart. I began to resist, to rationalize, to fall back into old patterns. As an alternative, Dr. J. suggested that I open up a conversation by asking my mother to tell about her childhood and growing up. Ah, I could manage that, I felt.

For as long as I could remember, Mother had told me stories about her life growing up on a farm with six sisters and one brother in the early 1900s. I knew that the family held some secrets about a tragedy surrounding her mother (my grandmother) and that her youngest sister (my aunt) had met an early death. But she had been vague about the details. As a youngster, I had not sought additional information. It was time to seize the moment, to unearth family stories and reinvigorate a dormant curiosity about my heritage.

I telephoned Mother and told her that I wanted to learn the details about her past, and asked if she would be interested in telling me some of the history. I also inquired if she would be willing to have me tape record it. Surprisingly, she readily agreed. She would be happy to come to my home in the foothills of San Diego so that we could begin.

I breathed a sigh of relief. I had not been a devoted daughter. Although living in the same general area, I had begged off from invitations to dinner with her and my father. We had not seen each other for nine months since Christmas time.

To begin our interview, we chose a warm September early afternoon. The morning coastal fog had lifted, transforming itself into wisps of clouds scudding across a cornflower blue sky. Mother arrived punctually as always. We hugged briefly and greeted each other warmly. We chatted about the lovely weather, as all strangers do.

The timing was ideal: My third-grade daughter was at school; my husband, at work in the downtown area. Our only interruption would be an occasional bark from our apricot poodle. I had prepared tea, and despite some initial awkwardness, we managed to exchange pleasantries. She wore an attractive blouse designed subtly with red roses. I knew that red was her favorite color, and I noted that she had taken special care with her appearance. I, too, had made an effort, hauling out the teacups with hand-painted flowers that she had given me when I married. For her, I had chosen the one with the red rose.

I motioned to the living room, and we seated ourselves facing each other. In these initial moments, each of us perched ourselves tensely on the edge of identical forest green velvet love seats. I held a spiral notebook and pen. The tape recorder sat on one of the two identical parquet nesting tables that separated the sofas. White filmy drapes, closed to prevent sun damage to the furniture, covered a bank of wall-to-wall windows with sliding doors in the center. A subdued glow suffused the room.

My hand shook a bit as I poured the tea. The cup clattered on its saucer as I handed it to her. Shyly, I met her hazel eyes flecked with green. Behind them was that calm, mysterious look that I never had been able to fathom. Realizing that we could use more light, I pulled the drapes partially and slid open a glass door so that we could enjoy the fresh air. Our home was built on a hillside so that looking west, beyond the deck, we caught a perfect view of the Pacific Ocean.

We sat staring at each other, with neither of us able to utter a word. The ocean was out there, miles away, yet seemed so near, so present. Gentle breezes carried in the scent of eucalyptus trees, caught the edges of the gauzy drapes, and lifted them into rolling billows, as if some über spirit had gathered up the ghosts of the past and blown them our way to conjure up our memories.

She nodded, and I turned on the tape recorder.

Part One—Revelation

Ye shall know the truth and the truth shall make you free.

—King James Bible, John 8:32

Unless we remember we cannot understand.

—E.M. Forster

Chapter 1

Madness

Too much sanity may be madness and the maddest of all,
to see life as it is and not as it should be.
> —Miguel de Cervantes Saavedra, in *Don Quixote*

Our first session opened with a question from me about my grandmother, Mother's mother. I knew she had been ill for a long time, but I had only learned recently through some cousins that she had been institutionalized with mental illness for over thirty years. With focused curiosity, I sought to learn what Mother knew about this. These are the opening words on the first tape.

It was her fears that did her in. My dad was on top of his religion. But my mother—she couldn't handle it. But that was according to their different dispositions. He was sure of himself. He was moral, and he taught all of us the moral virtues. He still had a firm religious belief, but he didn't ... well, he didn't impose a lot of that emotional stuff upon us. It was our surroundings, the church—no, the preachers, oh, those preachers!

Those fears ... I know that Mother was fearful of, well, you're afraid that you're not saved, you see. And you're frightened that if you commit a sin before you're forgiven, or if you die before you're forgiven, you'll go to hell. And if you get mad, that's a sin, and you should hold it all in. And oh, you're just admired like anything, you know, if you hold in all your temper and all your madness. And if you give into it, that's a sin.

Mother's worries were mostly religious, but I think they also were about insecurity, because she had this disposition—what would you call it? Non-self, I suppose, inferiority. Which I got full blown from her. She was a quiet sort without the will or training or advantages to be able to overcome this deep sense of feeling unworthy. And she didn't have the opportunities that I did. But I know that she had an awful lot of religious fear along with worry of insecurity, possibly apprehension about the future if something would happen to Dad. How would she raise us and all?

Of course, that was a realistic concern. There were eight of us kids, and women didn't work outside the home at that time. She couldn't have done anything. Anyway, to my mind, it was fear that put her where she was. She evidently coped with it until she was about forty-seven. Emma, the youngest, was born when Mother was forty-one or forty-two, I can't recall exactly. And after that, she began to worry and worry and worry, and get worse until she became suicidal.

She couldn't sleep and was walking the floor. I don't remember how long it was before she attempted to take her life. But I think it was bad enough that Dad knew that he had to be with her, and was afraid that she would ... .

I hate to tell you what it was—

(Long pause on the tape; Mother ducks her head, lowers her eyes, turns shy on me. I fear I will not hear the truth. But her reticence fades as she stiffens, looks up at me and speaks.)

She jumped in our well, our big open well.

I think it was July of 1916. Dad had been watching her day and night before that because I think he suspected that she might be trying to do something harmful to herself. And she couldn't sleep. I remember Dad and she took the mattress out in the yard to sleep. He was a strong man—you can't put it any other way. It was hot and steamy. So they were up walking around early one morning, and he told me later that he had walked out to the front gate for an instant to—I don't know what—left her for an instant, and saw her turn toward that well, and he knew what she was going to do.

To my dying day, I'll not forget being awakened by Dad's shrill voice, "Girls! Girls!" We knew what had happened. We knew because we had to hide the knives and scissors. We knew because my sister Frieda had caught her once with the lye. That call from Dad ... we just knew. It was in the early morning and we kids were all asleep. I know Carla was awake. She was my oldest sister, and she was walking toward her husband's farm, about three miles away. She had stayed with us for a while after she was married. It was the custom. They must not have been married but a week or two. But her husband sent for her to come to their honeymoon home, I guess. And she heard about it on the way. One of the neighbors told her. But I think the younger children—Carl, Gretchen, Margaret and Emma—slept through the whole thing.

Anyway, the water was deep enough that she could have drowned, maybe ten feet or so. It was a thirty-foot well. We had to draw water from the well, and it was at least twenty feet before the bucket hit the water. So that's how far she fell. Whether she got water in her lungs, or what, I don't know. And how it came not to kill her, I can't explain, because she jumped in headfirst. You see, it was a dug well. And there was this rock sticking out from the edge of the well, is the way I understand it. That's what she was holding on to. She would have drowned otherwise because she couldn't swim. She was staying herself on the rock, so that the water wasn't over her head. Now if her head had hit that rock, it would have been curtains.

Once we were roused by Dad's call, the three of us older girls ran down the stairs and into the yard. I could hear my dad calling down to her, "Are you all right?" And she answered, from way down inside that well, "Yes!" The fall must have brought her to herself, I guess. You know when you attempt to do something and it doesn't work out, why everyone tries to get out of it, isn't that right?

My dad rushed to the telephone. You had to crank it. We had this country telephone line, and if you had an emergency, you start to ring and ring and ring, and that early in the morning, few people were up. So everyone in the community heard the ring, so they knew that when somebody turned that crank for half a minute that there was something wrong.

Once someone came on the line and said hello to him, I heard him tell what happened.

"Bring all your ropes and all your men! Bring all the strong ropes you can!"

Our good friend and neighbor, Aunt Em—she had been a midwife to my mother at the birth of all the children—came running from her nearby farm, about half a mile away, and when she got there she cried out, "Oh my God, Delaney, oh my God, Delaney!" She was so agitated that she flapped her arms like a bird about to take off, and I saw my father brush her aside. He put his head in the air and went about his business as if no one else was there.

So there she was, alive and talking and everything else, not hurt. This tall strapping boy from one of the neighbors pulled her up out of the well. I think they fixed a harness around him, and he stayed down there until both of them got hauled up.

There is this windlass that you wind. It's a rod-like thing and you wind the rope around the rod until you get the empty bucket up. Then you drop the bucket down by letting the rope unwind. And were those buckets of water heavy! Am I explaining it all right? When it hits the water, it fills up and you can feel the jerk, like a fish taking a line. And you start winding it back up to get your water. So they must have attached the harness to the rope, and that's the way they pulled her up. They must have been strong men to haul up that much weight—she weighed about 250 pounds, I think.

Obviously, we couldn't drink from the well after that incident. It was not a stone or brick well, only an open hole covered with boards. And we couldn't understand why Dad didn't take care of the problem. Anyone of us could have fallen in. I remember going out at night when there was ice, and you had to reach to take the board off to pull the bracket forward. I had to hold my sister's dress tail to make sure she didn't tumble in. Finally, Dad nailed that damned well shut! He should have done it earlier. There was a spring on our property, and Dad made us carry water from there.

The first time I saw her right after she came out of that well, she was devastated. It was the only time that I saw or heard her talk irrationally. And it was all religious. She said she was sorry she did it but that it was for the good of the cause. Evidently, she meant for the good of the religious cause. She didn't explain, but that's the only time I ever heard her talk about it that way. We kept her home for a while. But among ourselves, we had an unspoken rule that we never talked about it.

I tell you, you can hardly understand it. Because all the time she was in the institution, she didn't seem to have a psychosis. Nor was she insane. The item in the local paper described her as having been "seized with an act of insanity ... ." All of us suffered for that publicity afterwards, because it wasn't true. I think she had clinical depression. When she was committed, they called it "involutional melancholia" or "involutional psychosis." I think it has something to do with the menopause.

But from that time on, each one of us understood that someone was to be with her day and night. It's naturally not too pleasant to recall these things. But it doesn't bother me. It doesn't tear me up or anything. Because it's there. I know it happened, and I just accept it.

So you know when I tell you what I've gone through, and why I ... but I've thrown off all those things. I have conquered, used enough mental hygiene on those things. I used to dream of open wells or of a great big hole in the ground that someone wouldn't fix. But I haven't had a nightmare about that for a long time. I know why I'm dreaming that way, and I throw it out into the air and it's gone.

You probably want to know how long it took for any of us to observe any signs or symptoms. I can't remember too much about that, but she had been bad enough that Dad was watching her. And he told one of the older girls that she was like this before, when they were first married, that he was afraid she was going to ... well, they called it losing your mind. And Dad thought it was over religion.

She really didn't talk too much about it, but you know, you can observe things. She'd sing hymns and you'd feel like she was singing to comfort herself. She would say to us, "Oh, but that is sweet and comforting." And she'd keep on singing. You sensed that she was uneasy about things, that something was dreadfully wrong.

But before that time, she didn't seem odd to us. She seemed like a normal mother. Why to me, she was just fine. You could go to her when you had a problem, and she would hold you and comfort you. But I look back over my life and remember some of the things she said, and I now know.

I'll tell you about a fear that haunted her. She told me once how she labored under the fear that she had committed the unpardonable sin. I don't know whether you know what that means. I don't think that I do, exactly. But they talked in church about "quenching the spirit."

Now this is really hard to believe, but she told me that she thought that she would have been saved—oh, anyway, that her religious life would have been better—if she had been able to shout. You know what shouting is? Religious shouting, where they get all happy and jump around? They're considered the most religious ones, the ones that shout. They become worked up emotionally. I think they are in another world. They even jump over the backs of the pews!

Mother had a sister who died as a teen-ager, and she had this first cousin who shouted at the funeral. She was troubled that she didn't do the same thing. "I knew that I should have felt like shouting but I quenched that," she said. She regretted that she had been afraid to do it. So she thought that she had quenched the spirit and committed the unpardonable sin. I heard these things long before Mother attempted her deed of self-destruction. For a long time she had such a bad back that she couldn't go to the revival meetings, but it wasn't long before this happened, I believe, that she was feeling better and was able to go. Maybe she got worked up, I don't know. She usually got to worrying when there were these emotional revivals in church.

She kept talking about it—that she ought to shout. But she wasn't that type. She was like me, the type of person that doesn't like to be demonstrative in front of people. But she felt as if she ought to, you see. I can remember once hearing her in church service shout out, "Praise the Lord!" But I could tell she forced it out. She didn't want to call out like that, but she thought she should.

Over time, she sank into depression and despair. Having nine children didn't help matters, and she had to cope with the hardships of farm life. We didn't have running water, electricity or indoor plumbing. But we did have a "hired girl," and by the time each of us reached six years old, we older girls were getting meals and doing all the indoor and outdoor chores. By the time Mother made her attempt, I was sixteen, Frieda was seventeen, Irma was nineteen. Carla was twenty-one, but as I said, she left to go live with her husband. We girls did all the housework, so I don't think it was entirely the physical strain. Maybe the triggering point came when she was dealing with the change in hormones, although she was still in her mid-forties. What got to her most, I think, aside from her religious fears, was this terrible inferiority complex, which was not helped at all by Dad. He was Irish, quite self-confident, and he kept her down. He had a strong ego—I think that's why he chose someone pliable. Still, I know he needed it, with eight kids and a wife like that.

Of course, he had to have her committed. I think it was several weeks until Dad got the wheels rolling. Because there were controls, yes, even at that time. Doctors had to certify ... because people would send their relatives off to get rid of them and put them in the mental hospital. I remember seeing him cry when his favorite sister Ellen came to see us and say goodbye to Mother. Dad had to sign papers to surrender her to the county law enforcement officer. Though why, I don't know because she was so submissive, so compliant. And when Ellen left, why, he leaned up against the oak tree in the front yard and his whole big frame shook with sobs. He really loved Mother, I feel sure. And for all his gruffness, he had his soft parts. The sheriff came and drove her off in a wagon pulled by two horses.

❧❧

The telephone rang. The poodle barked. I pushed the "off button" on the tape recorder. It was time to end the first session. We agreed to do another interview before too much time elapsed. Our good-bye hugs were genuine, and I felt a surge of daughter-love and gratitude for this day together.

Nothing had prepared me for the shock of my mother's revelations. In the interview, she assured me that she had remained willing to talk to me about these things had I ever asked. She insisted that she had not kept them hidden on purpose. But I had not inquired, and she had not volunteered.

This afternoon, I had been the questioner, resolved to stay distant from whatever my mother told me, as a reporter attempts to maintain objectivity in gathering the facts. Yet I found myself alternately speechless or else sputtering out questions, totally forgetting my intention to remain aloof from involvement. No chance. There it was: my heritage and her sorrow.

After my mother departed, I removed my glasses, now speckled with salty granules, and laid them carefully beside the tape recorder. I returned to the green velvet sofa and sat for a moment—or was it an hour—unable to make the next move. An unexplained aura enveloped me. Still dazed, I finally arose and stepped out on the balcony. I slowly inhaled hoping to dispel an intense feeling of weightless unreality. Squinting, I saw shimmers of light dancing on the distant ocean, like pinpoints of memory that pulse and perish and return again, all in an instant.

Stepping back inside, I drew the drapes to cut the glare of the western sun. I floated to the front door forgetting to retrieve my glasses. In a blurry haze, I descended the steps outside our home and walked down the hill to the bus stop to meet my daughter.

Chapter 2

Family Tree

We all grow up with the weight of history on us. Our ancestors dwell in the attics of our brains as they do in the spiraling chains of knowledge hidden in every cell of our bodies.
—Shirley Abbott

As we proceeded with the interviews, I became consumed with curiosity about the factors that may have led to my grandmother's shocking attempt at killing herself. Questions led back to the families in which my grandmother and grandfather grew up. What follows is not exactly a genealogical history, but rather stories passed along about those two families.

My grandmother's name was Esther Bowman. She married Henry Michael Delaney, my grandfather. Esther and Henry had nine children. The older sisters were Carla, Irma and Frieda. Next came my mother, Laura Catherine, destined to become a middle child. Her brother Carl was next in line. He was followed by the younger sisters Gretchen, Margaret, and Emma. Tommy, born after Gretchen, died in childhood.

I don't know if I ever told you about my mother's mother, but she was from a fine, aristocratic family in Pennsylvania. Her name was Sarah Winger. She chose to marry a strong-headed German farmer by the name of Peter Bowman, who was my grandfather. Possibly she was attracted by his potential to be successful financially. But oh, the things she had to put up with! I'll tell you about that later.

Peter's mother—this would be your great-great grandmother —had the foresight to acquire not only one but two tracts of farmland, and this turned out to be quite intelligent of her, because they were underlaid with valuable veins of coal. I know a bit about her—she was a Quaker and went through her life using the traditional "thee" and "thou" in her speech. But she was also hard-fisted and ambitious enough to get along in the world. So when she bought these two tracts, she saw to it that she also purchased the mineral rights. I've been told that she drove a hard bargain with the former owner, holding out until she secured an agreement from him. So the heirs were able to cash in on the coal veins without selling off the land. Unfortunately, nearly all of Mother's share went to pay for her care in the state mental hospital, and there was next to nothing left for any of us kids.

So Peter brought Sarah—my grandmother—as his bride to this two-tract acreage and proceeded to farm the land, like all the rest of the men in the area. My grandmother bore him thirteen children, but lost six of them. She had come out of genteel circumstances and passed along her Pennsylvania Dutch housewifely skills to my mother and my mother's sisters. They learned how to sew, and they were taught good manners. My mother loved pretty things, but she didn't get many during her married life.

I loved visiting their place because the house was so clean and orderly. There wasn't a string on the floor or a speck of dust anywhere, nothing except spic-and-span order. Also, there was maple sugar, and it smelled so wonderful. We girls called it the "Grandma house."

Now, what I'm going to tell you about Peter Bowman needs to stay between us, not to be shared. I think you should turn off the recorder.

(At this point, I acceded to my mother's request, realizing that if I were to learn about some of the family skeletons, I had better take notes. Most of what follows came "off tape.")

Peter Bowman was an arrogant, domineering man. My grandmother and all of his family had to dance to his tune, had to listen to what he had to say, do what he told them to do. I've been told that he would find something interesting in the paper and bellow out, "Silence! I'm a-goin' to read!"

But that wasn't the half of it. I heard this story from one of my aunts, an older sister of my mother. My Aunt Lila recalls hearing commotion in Peter and Sarah's bedroom night after night. I suppose that she was resisting his advances. No wonder. She was probably sick and tired of bearing children, nursing and caring for them. And the loss of so many ... Oh, I shudder when I think about her enduring that marital rape night after night, with no way to stop him.

All this explains to me why several of the Bowman daughters were mentally unstable. I really can't say whether their father abused them, but as I look back, I wonder. Because here's another peculiar thing I can now share. I mentioned that Dad had noticed Mother doing "worry talk" in their early marriage, and I can remember this frown would come over his face, and instead of talking about Mother, he'd say, "I *hate* Peter Bowman!" I think he may have known a whole lot that he didn't let on.

Two of the aunts met early deaths. You remember that I told you that Mother had a sister who had died as a teen-ager? And that at her funeral, Mother thought that she had "quenched the spirit"? Her name was Catherine, and she died of what they used to call "galloping consumption." It's a form of tuberculosis. Another sister Prudence also died of the same thing four years later.

But several of the other sisters had psychological problems. So Mother wasn't the only one. Did you ever hear about her sister Rita? I learned about her story from one of the aunts. Rita apparently had strange eating behaviors and manic episodes. She got married, but around age thirty, took her own life—I can hardly believe I'm telling you this—by throwing herself down the family well! She drowned, but the family hushed this all up, so I don't know a whole lot about it. But isn't it weird? I didn't know anything about Rita's cause of death at the time of Mother's tragedy because it had happened the year before I was born. But later, when I did learn these things, I often wondered if Mother was trying to repeat Rita's act because she knew that Rita had been successful.

Two others developed mental problems later in life. One of them—this would be Aunt Margaret—came to live with my sister Irma and her husband for a while. She pestered Irma to death by saying she was "losing her mind." Aunt Margaret would say things like, "Don't you think you should hide all your knives?" It was my sister Irma who took charge of the family after Mother's incident, and she was plenty tough. She didn't have any tolerance for pity making. So she would answer Aunt Margaret something like, "Why no, if you want to kill yourself, go ahead and do it!"

But I guess Irma became convinced that Aunt Margaret was truly suffering from delusions and proceeded to get the legal work done to commit her to the same hospital where Mother was a resident. Later, the hospital released Aunt Margaret back to the care of Irma. I think Irma may have initiated getting her out because of her guilt feelings of having committed her in the first place. Anyhow, I was told that she didn't stay too long with Irma—she was a handful—because she went to a lifetime care facility in the southern part of the state. She surrendered her inheritance to this place, and that's where she lived out her years.

Then there was your great-aunt Lila, the one who passed along those hush-hush stories about her parents. She also had strange eating behaviors. She about starved herself to death. And here's an irony: She had to go to the county "poor farm," where she died days before the final installment of the coal sale from their farm was being distributed.

And I suppose I told you that Mother had eating problems also. I can remember her sitting at the kitchen table with her chin upended pouring a stream of maple syrup into her mouth. Both Mother and Dad were getting increasingly heavy. I recall that once during a shopping expedition to a country store, they were being teased and taunted to get on the standing scales used to weigh cattle or sheep. I'm sure some eyebrows must have gone up when they saw the results. Dad used his weight as an excuse not to do much of the work around the farm and hired out what he could.

I've been talking about the Bowman sisters, but let me tell you a bit about some of the sons. They were all different from each other. The oldest one was Adam, and at times he worked on our farm, often staying over on our back porch. My sister Carla told me in later years that Adam chased her around the yard when no one was present. But she could run fast, and I think she eluded him. I guess he was a chip off the old block. Now here's something else—truly gross. Carla apparently caught a glimpse of him in the barn doing something—I think you can guess what—to a sheep. Can you imagine? I can hardly speak of these things, yet I know they all happened, and I blame that old coot, my grandfather. Isn't it something that one rotten person can have such a generational impact?

Fortunately, not all the boys were like Adam. One of the uncles, we dearly loved. This was Uncle Thomas. He was sensitive, kind and considerate. He's the one that persuaded Mother to get us not to drink coffee until age twenty-one. We got a dime for each year we were "good" about that. Anyhow, Uncle Thomas had a way of looking at you and talking to you that made you think you were the only one in the room. I was so jealous that he'd like Frieda better than me, so I asked him, "Which one of us do you like best?" He was such a diplomat. I think he answered something like, "Oh, I like—milk the best!"

He saw me cutting up a chicken one day and remarked, "That girl is going to be a doctor or a surgeon." I was thrilled, and that's where I got the idea that perhaps I *could* become a doctor. I had to settle for second best—women couldn't aspire to such things in those days—but being a nurse wasn't all that bad. Anyhow, Thomas left home early to escape our grandfather's overbearing nature, and oh, how I missed him!

I do remember some lighter moments, so I suppose it would be in order to talk about some of them. This one's about Uncle Thomas. After he left home, he became a bridge builder in Virginia, and he met and married the woman who became our Aunt Bessie. She was about as prissy as they come. They had only one child they named Owen, and Aunt Bessie wouldn't let him say "urinate." No, he had to say, "Make a river." Bathroom words were not acceptable in Aunt Bessie's world. One time in the winter, that family joined us for a sleigh ride. Dad got the horses hitched and loaded us all in the sleigh, and he called out, "Here we go a–sleighin'!" And our cousin Owen, who was a small kid at the time, yelled out, "Yah, here we go a–shittin'!" You can imagine how mortified Aunt Bessie was!

Now, Uncle Billy was a good guy, a happy-go-lucky sort. I once boarded at Uncle Billy's place when I was teaching, and I had a fairly happy time there. That's when I saw him dancing a jig with a milk pail in his hand. He was jumping up and down, singing and dancing that jig, and you know what happened? He came down so hard on the floor that he swallowed his dental bridge! Good thing it wasn't too large. I told the family, and everyone roared laughing and repeated that story for years, how Uncle Billy thought that was the funniest thing in the world.

Then there was poor Aunt Alice. She got stuck with a lot of the in-house work, like I did. She was mild-mannered, and she took pride in the fact that she was a lady who would never say bad words. But who knows what she heard from her father, that unbearable grandfather of mine? But you can be sure that Grandmother Sarah taught her girls in the proper ways. During one of our visits to the "Grandma house," Frieda and I witnessed this scene. Aunt Alice had the job of feeding the calves, and she was heating mush on the stove. Some of it slopped over on the top of the range and started dribbling down the front onto the floor. Aunt Alice stood there, planted her feet solidly, clenched her teeth and said ever so slowly with a pause between every syllable, "Jack-ass squirt shit! Jack-ass squirt shit!" And she lifted the pot of mush from the stove, sailed out the door and heaved the whole mess—including the pot—into the yard. I tell you, Frieda and I nearly died laughing. Oh, forgive me for telling you this!

(*My mother's apology seemed as charming to me as her story. We broke into side-splitting laughter until the tears came. I said to her, "What's to forgive? It's hysterical!"*)

My grandfather—Peter Bowman—died in the fall of 1916, about three months after my mother's suicide attempt. He had accumulated quite a bit of wealth when he inherited his mother's two farms. I believe his estate was between $15,000 and $20,000. That doesn't seem like much now, but it was a sizable fortune at the time. What a shame that Mother's portion had to go to provide for psychiatric care and housing. But still, I'm glad that we had it to give for her needs because she had a comfortable room in the state hospital, and she probably escaped the low level of care given to many of the residents.

I've given you quite an earful about Mother's family. I know a bit about Dad's family, but not as much. His mother was a church-going person and apparently responsible for his conversion to Christianity when he was a young man. From that point on, he held strong religious beliefs and applied high moral standards in his life. He was a teetotaler and would not permit anything resembling alcohol to enter our premises. I am convinced that his mother's influence was the source of my father's best traits. Dad had four siblings, including one sister who became pregnant out of wedlock and thus brought shame to the family. It ruined her whole life. That's the way it was in those days. If you strayed, you paid the penalty, and you had no future. His sister's predicament played a part in decisions he made that changed our lives forever. He wanted to protect us by moving us out to that isolated farm. But nothing will ever explain totally the tragic turn of events that affected us so deeply, and as you can see, left a permanent stain upon the entire family.

৵৹৵

As she talked, Mother gave me fresh insights into the relationship between her mother and father. Knowing something about their families grounded me in understanding the dynamics surrounding my grandmother's growing mental anguish. Propelled into a life that became overwhelming for her, she no doubt turned to religion as a source of comfort. While her mind became increasingly centered on fears of being religiously inadequate, a host of other influences converged to lead her into emotional darkness.

On one occasion, we sat with an old photo album with a worn red velvet cover, looking at early pictures, some faded in blurry sepia tones. Memories surfaced, and Mother continued talking, this time about her own parents.

Dad met Mother while he was working on and off on her father's farm. He took to Mother right away. She was the type that could be dominated. The other girls—her sisters—said that he was all right but that his nose was like a mashed potato! It was the custom to needle people when they were courting. But you mostly kept it to yourself.

They married when Mother was around twenty-one. I don't think they courted long before deciding to get married. Check out this picture—that's your grandmother in her wedding dress. You can see how tall and stately she looked with her dark hair piled high on her head. Those high cheekbones—I've heard that she got those from her Cherokee great-grandmother. Did you know that we have that strain running through us? Irma has that same look. I think it's exotic. And look at Dad. He is slender and has a fashionable mustache. He's wearing a suit with a vest, and around his neck is a white silk ascot tie. I'm sure this is the most dressed up they ever were. Look at those smart leather gloves. If you look closely, you can see his watch fob. In those days, there was no tradition of wearing white at your wedding or having a reception. Mother made her own dress of soft gray wool. The vows were said in the church after the service. You were called to the front and asked simply by the minister, "Do you wish to come forward and be married?" When both of them said yes, that was it. After church, the tradition was that the bride went to the home of her parents, where she fixed dinner for everyone to celebrate.

I wanted you to know what it was like for her in the beginning of their marriage. First, they moved to the little town of Garfield, where Dad was successful as a storekeeper.

There were household conveniences there—gas to cook with and to heat the house, water from a nice pump in the yard. They lived there until I was five years old and Gretchen had been

Esther and Henry Delaney wedding 1892

born. But for some reason Dad got this idea of buying a farm, which a business acquaintance offered to sell to him. I suppose he thought he could make a go of farming. And he liked the idea of raising his kids on a farm where we would not be exposed to the evils of town life. He had these peculiar ideas. For instance, he made us carry a lantern with us when we walked home from church. He was afraid that some of the young swains might try to get fresh. Oh, how we were embarrassed to do that! I came to believe later on that one of the reasons he left behind his prosperous income from the store in Garfield and brought us to the farm was his over-protectiveness of us girls. To think that tiny Garfield was populated enough to corrupt us!

He should probably have not gone into farming, since that change affected all of us from that point on. One cold November day in 1904 we all climbed into a wagon and left—six of us by that time—bumping across hilly terrain onto a hilltop farm with not much to recommend it in the way of good farming land, either. How we shivered that winter in our new home—it had a leaky roof that couldn't be patched until spring, and there was absolutely no insulation.

Even under these conditions, Mother learned to be a good housekeeper and cook, to sew and judge quality fabrics. There was no clutter or litter in the first house, all of which she had to put up with when she was taken to this tacky farm where she encountered every inconvenience imaginable. We had the help of hired girls, and did a lot of the work ourselves, but the entire situation must have depressed her. But she kept on—valiantly, I see now—amid increasing disorder, growing numbers of kids, and an increasingly heavy burden of work. We had to use wood and coal to cook with and to heat the house, and we had to draw water from a well instead of having the luxury of a pump. I know she tried hard to cope with everything. She sang all the time, obviously to keep up her spirits—folk songs, popular songs, lullabies and mostly hymns. The neighbors told us that they could hear her singing when we were all at school.

Temperamentally and emotionally, she had other factors to deal with. She was of a systematic, orderly temperament, and coping with all of this household chaos was confusing and difficult for her. As I mentioned before, she was also plagued by this residue of religious fears, which she had failed to resolve. But one of the most difficult parts of her life was that she met constant emotional abuse from Dad in the form of criticism and esteem-shattering remarks. The congruence of these things makes it easy to see that a crisis would erupt at some point.

There was another thing—despite the fact that she gave birth to nine children, I suspect she had her difficulties with sex. She told me in later years that she and Dad did not consummate their marriage until six weeks after the actual wedding ceremony. I guess the reason was those puritanical beliefs taught to her by her mother—that sex was a sin, and that you should not have sex unless you wanted to have a baby—nothing about marriage enjoyment. It was in the culture, the teaching of girls. I know we got the same messages from the aunts, Mother's sisters. And also, she must have heard the screams and pleas of her own mother, who was being abused constantly. That couldn't have helped. Oh, how mixed up she must have been! No wonder she turned to religion as a solace.

You might be thinking, why did they have so many children? I'll tell you what I learned. I'm being up front with you, because you asked. I hadn't planned to talk about any of this, but somehow you've opened up a floodgate of memories for me. Actually, Dad wanted to limit the family, probably by withdrawing, which was about the only form of birth control available for those isolated in the rural life. But it was Mother who felt that it wouldn't be doing God's will. In that sense, I think she sowed the seeds of her own destruction. It's hard to understand.

As for Dad, I got to wondering later in my life about the sarcasm he directed to me and the work he piled on Irma—was that the result of a lot of sexual tension? One baby after another came so fast that after a while, he didn't have someone lying right there by him. After Mother went to the hospital, I often wondered if he had a friend on the side. He met a number of various women over there—he talked about different women.

Nancy Key Roeder

And if that were so, I guess I couldn't blame him. He was still in his forties when this happened to Mother.

I strongly believe that Mother's trouble was clinical depression rather than a true psychosis. She never did lose touch with reality. To the day of her death she talked sensibly, intelligently and rationally. I know this because I lived at home and visited with her in the hospital quite a bit during the years before I went to nursing school. At one time, with the help of a psychiatrist, she made a partial comeback and was able to return home for about three years, but she couldn't quite hold her ground and had to be re-admitted.

In Dad she got a mixed blessing. He was good to her and no doubt respected her feelings a good bit of the time, and his Irish confidence bolstered her weak self-esteem. But his miserly attitudes toward money and his increasingly grouchy disposition fed her growing depression.

It was clear from the beginning that Dad ruled the roost. His word was our law. No matter what, he was always right. At least that's the way we came to think about it.

Did I tell you about the cat? It was just a barnyard cat, but I loved it. It belonged to all of us, but I thought of it as my special pet. Nothing more than a fluffy gray and white cat, not anything unusual. But the cat had been eating our chickens, and one day when we kids were playing outside, he caught the cat, held it upside down by its tail, then walked out to the oak tree and flung it, and—oh, I hate to remember this—whapped it over and over and over, against that tree, until it was limp and lifeless. And Dad dropped the cat at the foot of the tree as if it didn't matter at all to him and walked back into the house. All of us girls were frightened, but it didn't seem to mean a thing at all to Dad. We did not speak to each other about the cat after that. Because we couldn't do anything, and Dad told us that we had to sell the chickens for cash or else kill them for food. Frieda and Carl and I held a little ceremony for it, and then we buried the cat.

One thing that got to Mother, and I guess all of us to a certain extent, was my father's penny-pinching ways. They were really extreme. Once he promised Irma and Frieda a quarter to strip the wool from a sheep infested with maggots. It was a noxious job and they completed it, but they were never able to collect the promised money.

Here's another instance—the story of getting our teeth fixed. We learned about the importance of good dental hygiene in school, but we were not allowed to go to a dentist. Dad did not believe in them. He thought they were in it for the money only. But Frieda particularly—she was more successful with him than the rest of us—convinced him that we all needed to be seen. So he gave in—sort of—but insisted that any dental work would have to be paid for with the meager pennies we earned by picking up nails from around the farm. So we turned over what little was in our purses to him to help pay for the dental care. For a couple of us, it was almost too late. I, for one, lost a couple of my molars, and that's why I need to wear a bridge.

And there were my eyes. Did I ever tell you that when I was in high school I had to have my lessons read to me because my eyes ached so badly? I knew I needed glasses, but Dad wouldn't hear of it. I bathed my eyes and did exercises to try to improve things. I guess he was finally convinced I needed to see someone. But he warned me, "See you don't go to an expensive eye doctor." Frieda took me in, and once I had the new glasses, I put them on, and oh, how wonderful to see clearly! That doctor said he couldn't believe what a blur it had been for me all these years.

Once each of us graduated and found our first teaching jobs, Dad promoted the idea that each of us should borrow $50 each from Aunt Margaret—she was the banker in the family and she made it known that she had money to lend at interest. This would tide us over until we got our first check. It didn't occur to us to question Dad on this—that he could provide a bridge loan without interest to us, or support us until we got jobs.

That was Dad. We knew how he was. We were young and could take it, but I really felt for Mother. Dad put unreasonable budgetary restrictions on her. And he complained a lot— "growling," I called it. He would mutter about the size of the grocery bill, what Mother had bought or what she had *not* bought. He was never satisfied nor did he ever compliment her on her efforts to keep down expenses. It's a terrible memory, but I can still hear her crying for a whole morning. "I couldn't help it," she'd say to us with a tear-streaked face. "I had to buy food and this and that." Oh, how happy we were when she would wash her face and stop crying! And she would start singing those hymns to herself, to soothe her hurt feelings. But you know, I think at times he felt sorry about his actions—I can still see them going on walks together, hand in hand.

I don't think things were as bad financially as Dad made them out to be. He held the purse strings and didn't share any of that part with any of us, but as I look back, I think he just wasn't fair. We raised sheep, and when World War I broke out, wool brought a fine price. And he bought and sold several country stores during the "farm" years, all of which had been profitable.

I've often thought in retrospect that Dad's strong personality turned out to be a beneficial trait, for as things transpired he needed a stalwart will. My own emotional response was that he was a domineering, unloving, uncaring lout, who cared nothing for his family or individuals in it except as objects to satisfy his love of domination and control. He often mocked me much as he did with Mother, and he mimicked my speech. He made fun of me in front of the others, and I felt humiliated and worthless. But he wouldn't dare do that with Frieda or Irma. He may have thought he saw too much of Mother in me and wanted me to change, I don't know. Whatever the reason, I lived with all that until I could get free of it. But that's another story, for later.

It wouldn't be fair to Dad to let you think that he didn't have his good points. He certainly did. He demanded that we be scrupulously honest and morally straight. He was a pillar in the community and served as a president of the Board of Education for a number of rural schools. He established a church in our community. It's still there, along with the cemetery, where some of the family members are buried.

They say that there are sins of the heart and sins of the disposition. When I think of the ways in which he did show that he loved and cared about his family, I have to say that it was not a sin of the heart. For, unlike some men heading large families, he did make sure that we got the best education that was obtainable under the circumstances. He had a good mind himself, and he yearned for us to improve ours. Educating girls wasn't considered to be important at that time, but I think he realized that we all performed well in school, and saw to it that we could go to high school. He was so proud of any of us who received any honors. And when we got sick, he would panic and speedily call the doctor.

It would have been so easy to—and this is part of my tribute to him, too—do what some men did if their wives went off mentally. They would put them in the hospital and simply abandon their families for good. But Dad wasn't that sort of person. After we moved, he took a job right there in the hospital as an orderly in order to support the little kids who were still at home, and so that he could be near Mother and take her out whenever possible.

I've really struggled with my negative feelings about Dad. It took me a long time to get over the idea that he rejected me in favor of the other girls and especially of our brother. I once found it hard to forgive him for the way he treated me. But I hope I have given you a balanced picture. I guess I had to get away from Dad, to look back and give him credit for keeping the family together after Mother's tragedy.

Chapter 3

Family Prayer

Fear has many eyes and can see things underground.
        —Miguel de Cervantes Saavedra, in *Don Quixote*

As I mentioned, Dad was both a farmer and a storekeeper. One of the stores was at a railroad stop, miles away. There was not a village or town there, only a few buildings with a few apartments on the top level. During the week, he left all of us on the farm to do the chores. He was keeping the store, and he took Carl, my only brother, with him. Carl was not allowed to help around the house. That was women's work. So, Dad was around only on weekends. But I think he began to realize that he needed to be home with Mother. So Dad sold the store when he realized she was getting so bad. At least, I guess that's why.

During this time that Dad was away during the week, I got concerned because we weren't saying a blessing before our family meals. I think I was about seven or eight at the time. I had begun to be awfully influenced by those preachers—oh, those preachers! They told us we should have grace before meals and family prayer at night before going to bed. I thought that was our duty and all, that these were the requirements of being a good Christian. So one day during the week, while Dad was gone, we girls—and I kind of spearheaded it—agreed that we would have grace at the table, and that we would have family prayer every night. At first Mother went along with it, and we were banking on that to keep it going. Dad came home that weekend, and we gathered around. One of us read the Bible, and one said a blessing before eating.

He didn't say much that night one way or another. But we could tell he wasn't pleased. But the next day Mother told us, "Papa thinks he's the head of this house, and if we have family prayer, *he* is the one to decide to have family prayers." Oh, was

I crushed. Oh, I thought, how could he? How could anybody be that ... ? I knew it was the right thing to do, and he was a Christian, and he was religious. How could he? It was an awful heartache at the time. It's one of my lingering emotional scars.

This was right around the time that I began to become anxious and fearful for the salvation of my soul. When I was younger, there was comfort, not the kind of fear that grabbed me later. Because, when we were little, we four oldest kids would kneel beside Mother and pray, "Now I Lay Me Down to Sleep." To me, that was saying a prayer—reciting your prayers at night. And that takes care of it.

But as I grew older, I was taken in by all the religion. And I internalized it deeper than the rest did. But, you see, I didn't have any way of knowing anything else. Mother for the most part didn't lay too many trips on us, not like the preachers, but I do remember this one thing. I had burned myself on the stove, and it made me mad, and I, ooooh, I flew into a tantrum. You may not know it, but I had quite a fiery temper!

(*Having borne the brunt of that personality trait innumerable times, I sought not to dissuade her from this observation.*)

She said to me, "Laura, I would be afraid if I were you." And I knew what she meant—that I should be afraid that I would go to hell for expressing my anger. It was my childhood fear, being in terror of death, and that I wouldn't be ready. You know, ready for the coming of the Lord.

Around the age of eight or nine, I started sleepwalking. I think it was because I was in mortal fear of not being saved. I did a lot of daydreaming, and I worried a great deal about everything. My head was in the clouds, thinking about religion.

The preachers—they were like Billy Sunday. I guess you've heard of him. He was considered sensational. And Dwight Moody after him. But I didn't have a chance to hear any of those. They were in the large cities, you see. We were out there on a farm, really isolated, way out in the rolling hills. But the ones we had—they got to us.

There were these church meetings, all the time, at least every two weeks when a traveling evangelist would come and preach at our community church. They didn't talk too much about what the sins were—except using alcohol and losing your temper. But mostly, it was all about the "shoulds" and the "oughts," and that you should get saved. Grace at the table, prayers with the neighbors, that sort of thing. I knew how I was supposed to feel, but somehow, deep down, it all didn't seem authentic or real to me. I worried terribly because I didn't go through the kind of religious experience that I was supposed to. That's what I wondered about, why I fretted! I went forward at those meetings when the preachers called for people, but I still didn't truly feel anything very spiritual, so inwardly I thought I wouldn't be saved.

Not only that, but I hated what I had do to be saved. At one meeting after I joined the church—I was now a saved one—the preacher called the Christians to come up first. But the sinners were back in the audience, and you were supposed to talk to people at their seats. I despised it! But I *made* myself do it.

Here's a vivid memory. One of the ministers told a story about a little girl and her father. She became a Christian, and her father who was a non-believer, I guess, turned her out of the family home. But she would be all right and be cared for because of God in heaven. That was the same preacher who said that we should go to the neighbor's house and hold family prayer. It took me years before I could actually say this to you—it was a bunch of junk, that's what it was!

As I mentioned, we mostly got these ideas from the preachers. But all of us echoed the convictions of Mother and Dad. They told us if we did something wrong that we would go to the "bad place." They called it that. If you weren't good, you'd go to the "bad man." They didn't use the word "hell." I guess that's the way they controlled the way we believed, that we should be good or the "bad man" would get us. I pictured the bad man way down under the ground in a great big long box—I shudder when I think of how afraid I was.

They seemed to be ashamed of using the name God or Jesus— they called him "the good man." I remember a remark while playing with my sisters, and we'd argue over who had the rights to some homemade toy or doll. And I'd say, "No, that's mine." The others would say, "No, that's the good man's, because the good man owns everything."

For a while, at church, I didn't know exactly what everything meant until one night, when I was around six years old I got the message at a revival that you're supposed to go forward after the invitation. It's called the altar call. Irma and Frieda both went, and I wasn't going to be left behind. I didn't realize what would be expected of me because I turned to Frieda, and she was weeping and moaning. I asked, "Why are you crying?" I didn't know you were supposed to cry for your sins, be forgiven and be converted, and if you did that, you were saved. You were supposed to be baptized after that. The Methodists would either do it by sprinkling or immersion. Frieda and I wanted to be immersed—because there was the general idea that immersion made you a better Christian or something like that. Anyhow, we were "dunked" in the country "crick."

Oh, they made a great huge service of it just for us—they planned ahead of time. Naturally, it was during the summer. I remember I was nine at the time. I'm sure that I didn't realize what I was doing, but that I simply wanted to do what the other kids did. So it was planned, and the preacher came, and the whole congregation gathered there with lots of people all around. We wanted to do what the other kids did, go there and be immersed, while everyone watched, on the banks of the river. Everyone was singing, "Shall We Gather at the River." Several others were baptized at the same time.

Now you'd think that the fears should go away because if you are really connected to what they are telling you, you would be ready because you are baptized. But I didn't figure that out. No, I continued to live in complete terror that I would commit a sin, that I would not be ready. I was so much like Mother. She had been baptized, yet she worried constantly that she wasn't saved.

Another fear was that the world would be coming to an end. This was a prevailing theme in our church services—it was this apocalyptic vision you hear about these days.

If I heard a strange noise in the house at night—oh, I lived in horror that the world was coming to an end and I would go to the bad place. I could actually see it, the world blowing up. The way I pictured it—I suppose it was mentioned to me this way—was that God was coming in the sky—what they think of as the Rapture, you see. I don't know how much fear the others had—I suppose they brushed it off better than I did on account of my disposition.

I didn't feel I could talk to anyone about anything, let alone these deep fears about religion. That was my trouble. I never talked about this. Some way, I don't know, I was different from everybody else. The thought that someone else might have those same fears simply did not enter my mind. I was too afraid to bring up the subject, so I just kept quiet.

Frieda often introduced me by saying, "Laura doesn't talk much." I probably should have told her that she made me feel ashamed. But I didn't. I just clammed up. There were days when I felt I should say something, and I did do that with a little girlfriend at school. She wanted to know all about what she had heard, so I told her about the world coming to an end, that it was supposed to burn up. As I described it all to her, I could see it. I could look out the window and see the fire coming to burn up the world. And I said to her, "You'd better be good!" I was certain that I was right.

So these were the beliefs in the family. And I think Dad went along with all of it, but basically, he thought if you were moral—such as not lying—you would be all right. I don't think he was afraid. But I began to have this fear that I wouldn't be ready. And that was Mother's fear, too, that she wouldn't be saved. This "being saved" thing—as I said, we got that from the preachers at the protracted meetings, those revivals. People were supposed to go to these meetings and be saved, get converted, join the church, read the Bible, visit the neighbors and do family prayer with the neighbors. I hated that thought, but I knew that I ought to do it. One night, I remember lying in bed in the same room as Mother, saying to myself, "I'll do it! I'll do everything, Lord, that you say." When I told Mother of my determination, she said, "Praise Him!"

All of this led to the Billy Dotson business. The Billy Dotsons were a family living over the hill across the "holler." They were slovenly and uneducated and had low standards. There were six boys and two girls. The girls used to help out and work in our kitchen. But the boys, when they grew old enough, would go to the next town to carouse and do all sorts of things, you know. One Saturday night they walked there and came back in a sad state. A teacher who lived in a house on the way told us that he saw the Dotson boys come by and oh, were they happy. George was one of the Dotson children and he was crippled. Some of his brothers were trying to help him home, and they were all tipsy. So this teacher saw them go by his house staggering, holding up George who limped along. And this teacher heard one of the brothers exclaim, "By Dod, we dot him!"

I was persuaded that this family could be helped by being with the Lord. They needed to learn that they shouldn't go into Littlefield and get drunk! So I went to Dad one day and told him that the Lord wanted me to go to the Billy Dotsons and have prayers with them. He pushed it off for a while, but the first chance he saw me when we could be private, he said, "Laura, I have talked to Billy Dotson about religion. I have tried to win him, and you don't need to take that burden on yourself. Billy Dotson knows all about religion."

To this day, I'm not sure whether my Dad really did approach Billy Dotson. Perhaps he was ashamed of my efforts or trying to calm me down. I guess that I was obsessed with these ideas. But what he told me gave me a satisfied feeling that the responsibility could be off my mind. It was one of the few times there was some rapport between us and that he actually helped me. Possibly he feared that I was getting too much like Mother. I'll never really know.

అఱఁ

During our conversation, I reminded Mother that I had once written a sketch about my first religious experience, the day I was saved. Here is my story:

"Jesus Cher-rist!" bellowed my father when he found me behind the revival tent stage, praying. "Where have you been, child?"

"Finding Jesus Christ, Daddy," I answered with newly found thirteen-year-old piety. "Please don't swear, Daddy." My father's own strict, fundamentalist beliefs did not keep him from belting out his annoyance once in a while.

My "counselor" in the back room had disappeared before my father found me. She had already given me a Bible and some little devotionals after I'd followed the rest of the converts. She told me to pray every day, and God and Billy Graham would not forget me.

Handsome, virile Billy Graham—that's really why I'd come to the revival. Secretly, I had hoped that he would notice me sailing down the aisle like a bride, swaying to the beckoning hymn, "Just as I am … ."

It was 1953 and the Reverend Billy Graham was holding a tent meeting in our city. I planned to attend with my friend Myrna and some of her friends, who had invited me to join them. Mostly, I was curious because of Billy Graham's fame. The plan was for my father to pick us up afterwards.

The tent was enormous and smelled like the circus except there were no animals. The ground was strewn with sawdust. Ropes dangled from hastily erected poles and braces. Hundreds milled around, but the ushers deftly directed them to benches where they would be seated for the service.

Rev. Graham's booming voice filled the tent in rolling tones. We are all sinners, Rev. Graham told us, but God, through his Son Jesus Christ, calls us to be saved. An organist played softly in the background through the talk, then rose the volume slowly when Billy Graham stepped aside momentarily. People swayed to the music. Many women and some men were crying. And when I thought my heart would burst with love for God and Jesus Christ and Billy Graham, out stepped George Beverley Shea, who began to sing in a mellifluous baritone so beautiful I thought the angels must be listening. Then there was a brief pause while everyone prayed silently until awakened by the strains of the hymn I adored—"Just as I am, without one plea ... ." From where I was seated on a bench near the back, I saw a group of men and women arise from the front benches in one body as if prompted by a movie director. They floated in unison to the front like a giant ark looking for a place to land on Mt. Ararat. They stopped at the foot of the raised pulpit where Rev. Graham had delivered his sermon, and like one gigantic eye, turned toward the sea of faces. In one gesture, as if on cue, they motioned with their arms and hands, inviting the audience to join the ranks of the saved. Come, come forward. It was the high point. It was decision time. Billy Graham and his lieutenants were calling all brothers and sisters to step forward for Christ. People began to shuffle toward the front. Some were weeping. Some were carrying Bibles. Some were humming or singing the now too familiar "Just as I am ... ."

I dug my toe into the sawdust and ducked my head bashfully. The congregants were swooning, but I was not—not yet. Deep down, it didn't feel right to be part of this crowd. All I could think of was being afraid that Billy Graham would notice how homely I was. My friend Myrna, to my left, tugged at my sweater and whispered, "Go on!" I shook my head. She couldn't resist, though, and leaving me behind, she joined the flock swarming to the altar. I felt momentary relief—escape—until a woman on the bench behind me took my arm and turned me around. She had an open Bible and began to read John 3:16: "For God so loved the world that He gave his only begotten son; that whosoever believeth in him shall not perish but shall have everlasting life."

Somehow, this resonated with me, and I awakened fully to this moment. I left my seat feeling disembodied and moved toward the stage. Billy Graham descended and talked personally to all of us—hundreds of us—who had taken this important step. The lights were glaring, the tent was glowing like an alien spaceship, and I was feeling so spiritual that I truly believed that God himself with Jesus Christ might appear right then and there in a blaze of glory.

By groups we were led away from the main arena to a little space behind the platform, the same place where circus animals were kept when the tent was employed for other purposes. Each one had been assigned to someone who talked to us about our spiritual beliefs. If we only would confess that we are sinners, we will be converted and be gloriously saved through the sacrifice of Jesus Christ.

I sat there mesmerized, learning the virtues of the saved life. Forgetting that my parents would be coming to take Myrna and me home, I listened raptly. Any sense of time was put on hold. As I sat there praying, giving thanks for my new status as a saved person, my father's hooked nose swam into view.

"Oh!" I looked at him with misty, starry eyes, freckles stretching across my beaming face. "I thought you would be pleased that now I have gotten religion."

I had not been raised without exposure to the Godly path. We attended church and Sunday school regularly. It was part of our routine, taken for granted. My father's own peculiar interest, the prophecies in Revelation, provided frequent dinner monologues, through which I fidgeted. My mother's take on religion—little did I know the struggles of her past—was about applying "abundant living" in our daily lives, and that seemed to make practical sense to me. But until the day that Billy Graham brought his crusade to our town, I had not ever felt especially religious, nor was I ever bothered by spiritual concerns.

Alas, it took me exactly one day for the doubts to seep in. The image of the handsome minister with the wavy, sandy hair faded rapidly. From what was I saved? What did my decision for Christ really mean? Was I obligating the rest of my life to religious work? What in the world was everlasting life? Would praying help me with that wretched science notebook? Could I tell Jesus Christ that I worried constantly about having freckles?

The Presbyterian minister from our church made a hasty house call. He had heard that I had made a decision at the Graham crusade and wanted to know, anxiously, if I had any questions about my faith. He was fat, with pig-eyes, and he squinted at me above folds of flesh. I assured him that he wasn't to blame. I told him that I was carried away by the songs and the sermon. I'd be back in his church next Sunday. The folds of flesh dissolved into a forced smile. He looked relieved.

Weeks passed. My doubts and memories ebbed and flowed. First, I worried that Jesus would find me unworthy for his flock. Then I swung to the other extreme and cast the whole thing aside as hocus-pocus. Feelings of shame and embarrassment swept over me for letting myself be so manipulated.

"Don't worry so much," advised my mother, who worried mightily about the family budget. "It's normal for girls of your age to have intense religious experiences."

"Read Revelation," directed my father, when he observed my furrowed brow.

"Read your Bible, attend church every Sunday and pray every day," read the literature I now started to receive from the Billy Graham Crusade. And send money, it urged, to keep us going, saving souls for Jesus Christ.

After several months, I was convinced that you were not saved unless you provided financial assistance to the Billy Graham organization. I knew that when the pamphlets stopped arriving in the mailbox, because I had no monetary way of helping out. Besides, I was already hoarding the few nickels and dimes that I earned from babysitting to pay for bleaching cream for freckles.

☙◦❧

My day with Billy Graham as a naïve, budding adolescent hardly paralleled my mother's encounters with old-time religion. But each point in time bore resemblance and touched us in remarkably similar ways. No wonder she sheltered me with great protectiveness from getting too carried away with religious fervor. But she recognized the light-hearted side of it all, and we shared a moment of laughter together.

Going to the Well

Chapter 4

"The Short and Simple Annals of the Poor"

Let not Ambition mock their useful toil,
Their homely joys, and destiny obscure;
Nor Grandeur hear with a disdainful smile
The short and simple annals of the Poor.
                    —Thomas Gray, 1750
                        Portion of "Elegy Written in Country Church-Yard"

My mother and I sat one day looking through photographs, both
old and new. This particular recording session took place soon after
I had returned from a reunion of cousins, the children of all of her
sisters and one brother. One of the cousins took us on a trip to find
the old farmhouse, which still is standing. I was able to get a picture of
the side of the house. People were living there, and we did not want to
intrude upon their lives so we limited our picture-taking opportunities.
But enough is visible to match it with a faded photograph in my
mother's album. The two photos leave no doubt that the structures in
my photo and in hers are one and the same.

In Mother's picture, standing in front of a weathered farmhouse
behind a long picket fence is my grandmother, her hair piled high in
a bun. In one long row across the front of the house and stretching
around the corner is her brood of eight. She holds the hand of the
youngest, who looks to be about three. This child is probably Emma.
My mother looks about thirteen. That would be right since she was
ten years older than Emma. All of the girls are dressed in crisp, white
starched blouses with ankle-length skirts or in tailored long dresses. My
grandmother wears a white blouse and long dark skirt. In all cases, the
blouses or tops of the dresses cling high around their necks, often with
interesting, decorated collars.

The house indeed looks simple—a barebones dwelling with wooden
siding, a peaked roof and an extension on the back, which appears
to be an enclosed porch. The pickets wrap around the house in all

Delaney family circa 1914.
Back row: Irma, Frieda, Esther, Carla, Laura. Middle row: Gretchen, Carl.
Front: Margaret, Emma

directions, snake away into the distance and disappear in what seems to be an orchard. The fence leans toward the house as if the pickets need further support. My picture shows only the remnants of old pickets. It appears that the old fence has come down or has been taken away.

Although the houses in the two pictures show little differences despite the eighty years separating the two photos, one item in mine could not have appeared in hers: a television antenna. Using the photo to recall memories seemed to make it easier for my mother to speak about life on the farm.

Our house was smaller than some of the other farmhouses. And we didn't have a parlor like Aunt Em did. We felt less prosperous—our farm was not as productive as some of the other farms, our house was not as large, and our family was larger than those of the neighbors. In the living room, Mother insisted on having a rag carpet like the ones she was used to while growing up. We saved rags until we had enough to braid together to make a carpet. I remember the carpet balls, pieces of leftover fabric from sewing, flannel used for sheets, worn-out pieces of clothing like Dad's work clothes. We managed to produce one large enough to cover the living room. For padding we used wheat straw. We'd change it out about once a year. But our kitchen floor had no covering at all. The uneven pieces of wood were placed helter-skelter with wide cracks in between. I remember scrubbing it—you used a scrubbing broom and swept the dirty water on in front of you out the back door.

There were lots of tramps at that time, and they could come along and ask for lodging. We'd give them something to eat—we weren't afraid of hobos—but Mother would refuse them a place to sleep overnight. She would say, "Sorry, we have a large family and a small house." My little sister Gretchen, at age three, picked that right up and trotted out to greet any peddler that came our way. She'd tell them, "Sorry, you can't stay because our house is big and we have a small family." She got it twisted, but secretly I wished she'd gotten it right.

Once the aunts sent us coats. They were way out of style, and we got kidded at school. Mother had gumption at that time—and a slight sense of humor—because she told us, "Just say that every winter we get a barrel from the poor farm." So we made do with what we had and didn't moan about it. You might say we didn't have much of a choice.

We had no electricity, no running water, no indoor bathroom. But we did have a telephone. There were phone lines with these enormous batteries on top of the telephone poles. I'm thinking that electricity came in after we left. I guess most of it was done during the Depression by the Rural Electrification Program in the 1930s.

You mentioned how nice we all looked in that picture. Mother did see that we had good clothing. She would buy bolts of cloth about once a year, and sometime later take one or two of us to Maggie, the seamstress. Red was my favorite color and I remember one of those dresses. It was made of beautiful red wool, with an overblouse. The labor cost more than the fabrics, so Mother believed that you might as well get decent quality fabrics. We had only a few dresses. Most of the school things were gingham or calico, but she'd buy silk and taffeta to make our Sunday dresses—in summer it was organdy or dimity.

In addition to the clothes that Maggie made, we also sewed for ourselves. Each of the older girls taught the younger ones on our old treadle sewing machine. As we got older, we could do our own blouses. We also made bloomers that looked like skirts to hide our bodies—it was thought to be terrible to show your bust or your figure.

Shoes? We each had only one pair, so we had to wear galoshes over them in snow and rain. They were all high tops, and it seemed to take forever to lace them up. You had to wet the string like threading a needle. There were no plastic tips at the end to make it easy for you. Our stockings were not silk or nylon, but black cotton ribbed—knee length. We held them up by homemade "garters," simple and plain elastic bands. In summer, we didn't wear shoes at all.

We had vests for tops, no bras but something we called a shimmy shirt. For winter, we wore long johns—you'd freeze if you didn't! We made our own panties, and they had buttons at the sides but no elastic waistbands. On top of the drawers, for our Sunday dress up clothes, we wore corsets with bones and staves—can you believe this now? Mother ordered them from Sears-Roebuck. I guess that came down from the old idea that women should have small waistlines. Doesn't that originate with the idea of the chastity belt? Anyhow, between the supporters for hose and corsets under Sunday clothes, we could be rather uncomfortable at times. Everyday wear was more forgiving.

How did we get all those clothes washed? Not easily, I'll tell you. As you can imagine, doing the things that required water took quite a bit of effort. For one thing, we made our own soap for washing clothes. It had lye in it and smelled bad. In addition to our piles and piles of dresses, skirts, underwear and stockings, there were Dad's overalls and Carl's clothes, too. I can remember scrubbing things clean on a washboard, piles and piles of clothes and stockings.

We did the clothes once a week. It went something like this. We built a fire outside and set out at least three tubs and a washboard—one tub for washing, one for rinse water, one for bluing or starching. We didn't have to get all of our water for these chores from the well because we caught rainwater in a bucket—oh, did we have fun shouting down the rain barrel! We'd whittle the cakes of soap into the tub that held the washboards. We'd rub the shavings into the clothes while getting everything ready for the boiling. The boiling kettle was also the apple butter tub. Once the water boiled, the clothes got transferred to this pot. We added soap, took a broomstick, and twirled the clothes out of the boiling water and into the rinse water. We'd change rinse water for each bunch.

We had to wring out the clothes by hand—they would have been too hot in the boiling water, so we'd wring them out of the rinse water once or twice. The next tub was bluing. That was cool water. The bluing makes white things whiter.

Finally came the starching. We starched things like dresses. Without starch, ironing was hard. Our Sunday clothes definitely got starched, but not our flannel school clothes. We made the starch from flour. It's hard to the keep the lumps out—they would appear in your clothes. Argo was the first manufactured starch. Wonderful!

We used a wicker wash basket to hang the clothes on the line. In winter, it was too cold to wring them out, so we hung them dripping wet! But that could be a problem because in freezing weather, they can break in half if you bend them. In the coldest part of the winter, we couldn't do the clothes, so they piled up. Our clothespins were not the spring type but instead the kind used to make clothes pin dolls. You had to work hard to secure the wet wash on the line. And when storms blew in especially in the summer, you'd have to run and gather the clothes and haul them into the house. When it stopped raining, you'd have to go out and re-hang them all.

For washing dishes, we used that same homemade soap. You rub it off into the water in order to do the dishes. I remember when washing powder like Dreft came in. I think it was introduced at the World's Fair in San Francisco—that was in 1915—but we didn't have that for a good long while.

As for bathing, that was what you'd call "primitive." Our bathtub was an old iron corrugated washtub sitting in the kitchen beside the stove. We'd heat the water and put it in the tub and shooed everyone out. We each got a bath once a week, but between times, we were required to wash neck, ears, face, head—the parts that showed.

People don't iron much now since wash and wear has come in, but ironing was a big deal for us. We did it at the end of the eating table—there was no ironing board. The iron itself was a solid block of real iron. It was smooth, with a type of curved handle. We lit a fire on the stove and had to juggle keeping the iron hot along with taking care of the fire. We rested this hot block of metal on several layers of folded up cotton flannel, sort of like an early-type hot pad. One iron we used had a removable handle. When you went to heat it again, you took off the handle, and oh, did it get hot! You had to use some protective covering for your hands. Can you believe that we ironed not only our dress clothes but our underclothing also?

We four older girls did all the washing and ironing. Carl was not allowed to do women's work and Gretchen was too little. Carl played most of the time. Maybe that's why Dad bought the store, to take Carl with him and teach him something, I don't know. But he wouldn't let him do housework.

Oh, I do remember one thing Carl had to do. He had a little red wagon—Dad made sure that Carl had all the "boy" things—and pulled it around over the farm to get wood for the wood yard. That was a place outside near the barn where the wood got stacked. I remember the woodpile. Dad chopped down four trees and cut them into lengths for the firewood for the stove. We girls had to chop up what he found into smaller pieces for use inside the house.

We also had a coal pile. It was in back of the wood yard. We'd shovel the coal into a coal bucket, which had a spout to pour the coal into the fire. We'd use a poker to poke the fire or break up the coal. Dad got the coal from the railroad where the railroad cars came through filled with coal. My sisters and I would carry the coal and the wood inside. Carl had to keep the wood box full, that's all. But we girls had to chop up the kindling at night, even if it kept us up until midnight.

You might guess that the farm was the ultimate recycling facility. That was due to our conditions of poverty, but also because Mother and Dad taught us the highest level of frugality. I recall that a box of matches to light the lumps of coal cost five cents. To save matches, Mother made pipe lighters by rolling paper in strips to make a lighter. We kept them on the mantel, and instead of matches, we used those pipe lighters for the wood fire in the stove and the coal in the fireplace. We also used them to light the kerosene lamps.

You're probably thinking that our household was all work and no play. But that's not the case. We had good times as youngsters and growing children living on the farm. We played games with each other—parlor games like Fruit Basket Upside Down. We were elated the few times Mother and Dad played with us. But they usually just sat in the living room and watched us at play. I realize that they worked hard and were often tired.

Toys were scarce, but we had marbles, only one each. We also built little wagons by putting "wheels" on a little box—they were the tops of tin cans. We created our own Flinch cards because we had seen one set at a friend's house, and we proceeded to get some cardboard and make the cards ourselves.

My older sisters and I lived out our childhoods before the era of movies, but had there been films, we lived too far away from a town. No, we had to dream up our own entertainment. I can remember doing plays at school. Those of us taking parts would meet at night and practice for an hour or two. We'd string up curtains across the front of the schoolroom and invite an audience. We didn't accept any pay because we felt like performing for the joy of it.

As for other entertainment, we had to make up our own, use our own imaginations. But we had each other, and that helped. We made dolls from cornhusks and clothespins. Once I cut out what I thought to be a fancy wardrobe for my cornhusk doll, like one I'd seen in the Sear-Roebuck catalog. I was so proud of it until I tried to dress it and found that what I'd created didn't fit! But Frieda showed me how to cut out scraps of cloth the right way. We'd dress them up and have mock burials—we would bury Peter Dickens or Daisy Mason. Who were they? Oh, I don't know, names we made up! But we'd sing and pray and bury them properly outside. We'd also play "preacher" and fight for our chance to do the sermon.

We learned outdoor games like "base," a form of softball but with no ball or bat. We weren't totally isolated. People gave parties, and there were church picnics and ice cream suppers. Sometimes we'd have overnight guests, relatives or friends— honestly, I don't know where we put them—but those were fun times, and Mother let us make taffy. You have to cook it perfectly to make it pull. You have to get out the air bubbles, and Mother knew exactly how to do it. I recall one taffy party where we invited some young men. The next morning, we saw the taffy stuck all over our picket fence. So much for getting boyfriends out of that party!

To celebrate the holidays, we figured out ways to use the things around us. At Easter time, we kids had permission to rob the hen's nest. The night before, we hid the eggs all over the yard and some in the barn. We didn't boil them first. The next day, those who hadn't done the hiding got to find the eggs, and that's when they got fixed for breakfast. We'd take turns each year being the hider or the finder. Easter was one day that we didn't have to skip having eggs for breakfast. We could have two if we wished.

Fourth of July was really important in our family. Dad got flags and we put them all over, year after year. We'd parade around the yard banging dishpans with spoons and singing the Star Spangled Banner. We were all proud to be Americans and thought this was the greatest thing we could do to show our patriotism.

For Halloween, we did tricks on our own family—not bad tricks. One Halloween night we kids were playing around the barn. We fixed up a pail and suspended it way out from the barn on a broom. Then we called others to come see us, and we'd drop the broom so that the bucket of hay would fall on their heads.

At Christmas time, we had no evergreen trees, but Dad would go out and cut a small oak or maple with no leaves. We'd decorate it with popcorn balls and cutouts from magazines. The younger ones believed in Santa Claus. Every year we would recite "The Night Before Christmas" on Christmas Eve. I can remember doing that before we left Garfield. The older ones knew there was no Santa but they were careful to keep the secret from the younger ones. We didn't give presents to each other. Instead, the presents to us were tied to the tree. One year Dad bought Carl a tin whistle. This was when Carl still believed, and he called up the chimney the night before, "Hey, Santa Claus, will you bring Carl a tin whistle?" Those of us in the know really got tickled at that. It was exciting to run downstairs and get our presents in the morning. I remember seeing the only doll I ever got—it was from Aunt Lila—tied on the tree.

We generally had a better dinner on Christmas Day, and often candy. Mother and Dad portioned it out—divinity, fudge, ribbon candy. We'd have mince pies and one orange, something we never saw during the year. Dad would cut it in sections and divide them among the family. We were happy, and that was Christmas enough.

Oh, I must tell you about how we celebrated birthdays. They were important doings in our family, mostly because Mother made sure something special happened for each one of us. Upstairs, each of us had a small wooden crate with a top—we called it our "thing box." In it we kept a bunch of little treasures that we hoarded and guarded with our lives. Occasionally we'd get tired of our stash and trade with each other.

There might be paper dolls, or clothespin dolls all dressed up, a penny found or given to us, a special marble—you know, a shooter—or pictures cut from magazines. We had campaign buttons—old ones from the 1904 Teddy Roosevelt vs. Alton Parker campaign, and also William Jennings Bryan vs. William Howard Taft. That was the 1908 election. I had just turned nine, but Irma was old enough to be interested, and she didn't hesitate to make her opinions known. Dad was for Roosevelt, but Irma said she was for Bryan. Doesn't that figure? I really don't think Irma cared who won the election. She wanted to like whatever and whoever Dad didn't.

We also kept things from Sunday school—cards, pictures from our "Quarterlies" called the "The Golden Text." And we girls sported a breast pin, a small and round lapel pin with our birth date on it. Mother would buy each one of us one shortly after we were born. We refused to trade those; they were too precious.

Birthdays were special. When our turn came up, the night before, all of our plates were turned upside down, and we put something under the plate. It had to come from our own "thing box." The birthday person got quite a haul the next day. But as I said, we traded all the time, so sometimes—but not always—we got our treasure back. I think it was a good lesson in sharing, but I know that Irma especially did not want to let go of any of hers. She went along with the custom, but I'm sure she didn't like it. She was just that way.

So those were some of the ways we lived. I think of those childhood days of ours as "the short and simple annals of the poor." In later years, Irma had trouble getting over how terrible things were for us, but I didn't think of it that way. We all knew things weren't the best that they could be, but I took the work as a matter of course, especially in those years before Mother's tragedy. There were definitely advantages and pleasures connected with farm life. Things weren't all that dreary, and I'll save some of those stories for our next tape.

Chapter 5

In the Garden: Memories Caught

There is a garden in every childhood, an enchanted place where colors are brighter, the air softer, and the morning more fragrant than ever again.
—Elizabeth Lawrence

We called it Twin Oaks Farm. That's because of the two wonderful oak trees in our back yard. There weren't any others like them around our property, but I have heard Mother say—I don't know how she knew this—these two great oak trees were from the original forest that had been cleared off for farming. And there were apple trees galore! The previous owner had planted them so that each kind of apple would ripen throughout the growing season, starting in May, on through the summer into fall or early winter. We made pies and applesauce and apple butter—gallons and gallons of it—which we cooked in a copper kettle over an open fire we built in the yard. There was apple cider in the fall, but it didn't last too long. We made sure we drank it up before the hired men could get to it. They got really happy as it fermented, you see. On those crisp October evenings, Aunt Em would come over, and we'd all sit around eating raw apples while Frieda played the organ and we all sang hymns. I like to think that it was apples that got us through those hard winters. To this day, when the leaves begin to turn, I think of apples in our cellar and can still smell them and taste their tang.

The land was gently rolling—undulating you might say—and our farm home was on the top of all those hills. The lower end of the property, where the farm land sloped down to the valleys— that was the better soil. So the place that we raised potatoes and some of our corn was in the lower elevations because, you see, the dirt would wash downhill into the lower part and make it productive.

Something you asked about the community—I had not thought about whether there was a community, but I guess it was, more or less. We were there on a sort of ridge—we called it Clear Ridge—and it was like living on a plateau that sloped off on both sides to the railroad tracks, with some towns and villages on each side. We didn't know much about them. But surrounding us were neighboring farms, and I *would* call it a community because we all went to the same church, the same school, had the same post office, the same phone line. We had to go through Central to reach phones in other places. And we had the same grocery store, the same doctor, so all those things pulled us together. Everybody knew everybody else because we were linked in all those ways.

Our house was painted white with wood shingles. The roof was leaking when we bought it. Finally, Dad put on a galvanized iron roof. I can still remember hearing the rain drumming on that roof like horses clopping over all those wavy metal ridges. It was not really a two-story. The top floor was an attic because we could reach the ceiling, and that's where all of us kids slept. I think you could call it a story and a half. The front door led to the porch, which was crumbling. We were warned not to go there, but Dad finally fixed it so that we could go out and sit and catch lightning bugs in jars to light our way up the stairs in summer. When the cold weather set in, it was a different story.

There were narrow stairs leading to the attic. Somehow, we managed to get two bedrooms out of that space. One was quite large with two double beds and a cot, and there was another small one with one double bed. We had these bulky bedsteads, four posters. To hang up our clothes—there was no room for closets—we drove nails into the wall. Besides, coat hangers cost five cents each. We also strung wires across the end of both bedrooms and attached a piece of material for a curtain to have privacy in dressing. Our mattresses were simply flannel bags filled with straw. No innerspring mattresses for us—not until much, much later. Every year, we would empty them out after the wheat was threshed and put in new straw. We had quilts and comforts that we made during the winter. Comforts were made with heavier stuff and had knots—we'd save pieces of old clothes for them. Sheets? We had none. We slept next to quilts, which we washed often. We'd shave the yellow naphtha into a tub of water until it was sudsy, then trample our bedclothes with our bare feet. For pillows, we made cases to stuff with chicken feathers. When we killed the chickens, we plucked their feathers and dried them out. But the pillows got smelly fast, so we shook them out often and stuffed them again.

We didn't worry about it at the time, but I think we must have been living in a tinderbox. You know, Aunt Em used to worry about fire. In cold weather we'd use papers to start the fire and to burn the soot, and that sent sparks up the chimney. We didn't have a plan for survival. I suppose we would have killed ourselves if we tried to jump from the windows. We had to go upstairs in the dark—it was like midnight upstairs. But, if you can believe it, at night Mother and Dad let us light our way up those stairs with candles and matches. I never could understand why they let us take that risk. I guess they trusted us.

For a while we used kerosene lanterns, but not after we nearly had a fire with one. It was our only source of lighting at the time. We used them in the evening to do dishes and clean up from supper or read our school lessons. One night Gretchen and Margaret saw that one lamp was about to blow up. Somehow, kerosene had gotten too close to the wick. We were all in the living room, and Dad realized he had to do something. Margaret already had the lamp in her hand. Dad grabbed it from her, stomped to the front door and hurled it out to the middle of the road—about twelve to fifteen feet—past the porch. Margaret began to cry, "You ran against me. Why did you do that?" I guess it scared her to see how strong and decisive Dad was. As the older sisters, Frieda and Irma and I knew all about that.

The main level had a sitting room, kitchen, bedrooms. The living room held a grate for the coal fire. It was at the end of the room. Right next to this fireplace was a double bed—another four-poster—in the middle of the room, pushed up against the wall. That's where Mother slept with the babies. We didn't have cribs or cradles, no, she slept with them in her arms. And we didn't have a sofa, either, or anything where we could entertain folks who would drop by. It was too cramped with beds all over. So when we had visitors, we would bring chairs from the kitchen. We had no wall decorations, no art, but two things did hang on the walls—Mother and Dad's wedding picture and a portrait of President McKinley, which Dad bought from a traveling salesman who capitalized on the sentiment after the President was shot and killed. The words under the portrait read, "Gone but Not Forgotten." In the back of the living room, the entire width was a bedroom with a little step down to the kitchen. That's where Dad slept, and I think Carl, also, when he got older. There was also a small bedroom behind the kitchen. That's where the hired hands stayed over, or visiting relatives.

Our kitchen was tiny. The original stove had four burners and a small firebox, not handy at all. Mother begged for a new range, and Dad finally got her a really nice one—"Kalamazoo direct to you." It had a firebox with four burners in front and two further back, and it was twice as large as the old one. There was also an enclosed warming oven for things you had already served up for dinner. A lid pulled down at the back where it covered a reservoir for water that went the whole width of the range. We'd dip water out and didn't have to heat it separately as we did before. It had been so hard to regulate the temperature for baking in those older ovens. But this one had a clock-like thing, an early type of thermometer, with numbers one through seven. That helped a lot, especially for baking pies and bread and biscuits. Behind the range were a wood box and a coal bucket. There was a workspace shelf and a bucket of drinking water, a board to roll out pie dough and set the pan with kneaded dough for bread. We did put in a sink, but we had no running water, so there was a slop bucket—into that went the scraps from potato peels and all, and the cleaning up water. That's what we fed the hogs.

The table stretched the whole length of the kitchen. There was a long bench on one side. On the other side were four chairs, homemade with lattice bottoms. Two chairs were at the end. That's where Mother and Dad sat. Each of us had our place. We had to come to meals and eat together. Mother insisted on that. She also had us put a tablecloth on the table for each meal. "It's the decent and civilized thing to do," she told us. Dad said grace, mumbling some words. Dishes were passed around family style. Dad was strict. You put food on your plate, and you could not cut up or laugh—no jokes. There was some conversation, but Dad led it, no one else.

Breakfast might be fried potatoes or buckwheat pancakes with syrup. We made sorghum syrup because we raised grain. To make it, you grind down the sorghum and boil it down until it gets thick. We got sausage from ground pork and rendered the lard to keep in crocks in the cellar. We had eggs at times, or fried sowbelly and occasionally, ham. Dinner—we now call it lunch —might be vegetables, potatoes boiled with jackets on, with fruit in the summer, apples in the winter. Dessert would be bread and butter. We lacked protein, especially in the winter and because Dad rationed the chickens and eggs.

We did have a cupboard with several shelves for the dishes. We each had our own plate, refined crockery ware. There was a set of silverware, six of each. As the family grew, we pieced out the set. And we had a set of cut glass dessert dishes rimmed in 24-karat gold. Dad's sister gave them to Mother to celebrate my birth. Since I was the fourth child, I suppose it was really something special.

You used to wonder why I used so many dishcloths—I learned that from my mother. She wanted a separate cloth for everything, to wipe up the floor, to clean off the table, and there was a special linen cloth to shine the glassware. She tried to keep some of the refinement she had learned at home.

Mother had a bureau with one little dresser drawer where she kept the entire lot of her personal things. Besides a few undergarments, she had letters, cards, keepsakes. When she was growing up, the boys and girls would have parties, and you would make up cards the size of today's business cards. You would sign them and exchange them with friends, as kids today do with their yearbooks. We discovered all these things after she left for the hospital. Yes, we even found her love letters to Dad. She wrote about how much she honored him and wanted the right to tie his tie. I felt a little queasy reading them, like I was snooping or something, but it did tell me something about their courtship.

Mother and Dad didn't sleep together. She slept alone because she was always with a baby—and they were both such large people. But there was no locked door between the two bedrooms. And in the morning, why we'd often find that Dad was in Mother's bed. After I learned the facts of life—Frieda enlightened me—I told her, "Mother was in Dad's bed this morning. All right, now let's count nine months from this point and see if she has a baby." I hadn't figured it all out by that time. But Frieda said, "Well, it doesn't always take!"

Dad did his shaving in his bedroom with a bowl of water and a cup for his supplies. I suppose he kept business papers in that desk, too, and we also knew that he had a sword from his grandfather, who was in the Civil War. He also kept a revolver. He didn't keep it loaded—it had six chambers, but I never saw it loaded. The only time I remember him using it was when we had a dog that began to foam at the mouth. Oh, and one other time when Carl got bitten by a copperhead in the cornfield.

That time, they were baling hay—the hayfield is a nest for snakes—and Carl told Dad something stung him. Dad saw the fang marks on Carl's leg and cut through them to squeeze out the poison—they don't advise that now. And he ran back to the house, got the gun and killed the snake. He sliced it up and put the flesh on Carl's bite—I saw that white flesh turn green—and he sucked the rest of the poison out. Dad also tied on a tourniquet—you're not supposed to do that now because it could cut off circulation. That leg swelled a lot, but Carl escaped getting a systemic infection. As I look back, I realize that some of our survival was just plain luck.

Like all farm people, we grew most of our own food. We girls had to weed the garden with our bare hands—it's not any worse than hoeing corn. I didn't think it was too hard. There was an extensive potato patch—you'd cut a potato in pieces with one eye in every piece so it could sprout, then harvest the crop in the fall when the vines died. Since we didn't have refrigeration, we dug a great big hole in the back yard, deep enough to prevent freezing. You would pile lots of dirt over the potatoes and get them out by digging a little hole in the side to take a few out so the rest wouldn't freeze. We ate potatoes morning, noon and night. Like the apples in the cellar, we could count on potatoes to fill us up during the winter months.

The garden yielded plenty of fresh vegetables in the summer—cabbage, cucumbers, parsnips, sweet corn, huge juicy tomatoes. We had onions and lettuce, but we didn't ever put them together in a salad. I'm not sure we knew the meaning of the word. We chewed and swallowed the young onions straight from the garden. I know it sounds terrible, but we scalded the lettuce and put vinegar on it. Now why we didn't eat that fresh lettuce, I can't tell you. We didn't have pressure cookers until much later, so we couldn't preserve the garden vegetables over the winter. We knew about botulism and didn't want to take a chance. But anything with acid in it was all right, so our cabbage became sauerkraut—that's one vegetable we did can, by boiling the jars well. We put up pickles, too, using fresh cucumbers and tomatoes. Have you ever heard of green tomato ketchup? It's not at all like the bottled catsup available in the stores. It's made from cabbage and green tomatoes, the ones you pick before the frost arrives. You add a bit of liquid and cook it down, and add sugar. It was a great flavoring for our bland and simple food— really delicious! But now people don't have the time to mess with those preparations.

Do you remember when you were little, how you would help me cut up beans or shell peas or peel peaches for canning? Well, we did can fruit because we had peach, pear, plum and cherry trees. But during the summer when the peaches came in, we saved a lot of them for Sunday dinner. And we put up jams and jellies—oh, the taste of cherry jelly or plum jam on a freshly baked piece of bread slathered with butter! We worked hard to keep all of this going, but we didn't think of it as too much work—only Irma thought that.

Our wheat got harvested in the fall and stored in a granary. Dad took it to the mill in Littlefield in burlap sacks. The mill ground it and we got it back in paper flour sacks, with the hulls taken out. That's what we made the bread from. We'd bake twelve loaves at a time. I took over when Mother was failing.

I didn't think it was drudgery. Speaking of grains, we had corn, too. Dad took that to the mill to grind into corn meal. We had lots of corn meal mush with sorghum syrup, and we made cornbread, too.

We kept one or two milk cows, so that's how we got the cream for our butter. We churned it, counting the strokes each one did so we could take turns. We sold as much as we could. We were denied butter on occasion because of its sale value. As for the cows, I did most of the milking. You have to learn it. It doesn't come to you naturally. Carl never did learn how to milk. The cows wandered all over the farm, and I had to go get them. It didn't bother me to do that. I rather liked running through the fields and singing "Mary go call the cattle home." I remember writing poetry in my head while I raced out to the pasture to get the cows. I think I was about twelve.

Let's see, we had eggs from the hens, but Dad rationed those because we sold the eggs. When we did get them, we'd eat the fertilized ones—they're supposed to be better for you. The young chickens we would use for fryers. I was the one that had to go out and chop their heads off in the morning—they're hard to catch and they flop!

We raised lots of chickens. I would set the hens, that is, put eggs under the wings. They were scared of you, and when they were sitting on their eggs, they'd peck at you. I learned really fast how to avoid that. We kept a few roosters for obvious reasons. It took three weeks for baby chicks to mature. I thought it so exciting to hear the peck-peck-peck of a new chick breaking out of its shell.

The other girls didn't take to housework like I did, so I took over cutting up the chickens. It was a treat to have chicken for dinner. We boiled it and served it with gravy, steamed and plain. It was good enough, seasoned with salt and pepper. We'd cook several dozen chickens at a time in this big black pot.

When we got tired of chicken, we'd start on pork. Dad occasionally would slaughter a hog. Some of it got ground into sausage, but other times it got smoked into hams. We sold the hams and ate some of the other parts. But there's not much lean, if you can't preserve it. We took the fat and made it into lard through rendering. It first went into crocks, then down into the cellar where it kept cool until spring. We rarely got beef because we sold the calves for veal and kept the cows for milking. I do recall one time when Dad bought half a beef and hung it in the smoke house during a cold spell, where it stayed frozen. Our situation was typical—there was no ice delivery, no way to keep fresh meat. But once in a while an enterprising entrepreneur would come along selling ice. We'd hear his wagon jangling along and heard him call out, "Here comes the ice man! Bring your dish pan!" But that didn't happen often.

Our only contact with seafood was when Dad would bring back a half pail of oysters. This was only when ice was available. We ate them fried, or Mother made oyster stew. I didn't like the taste, but you didn't dare say so then. I can tell it now—I hated them!

One of my best-remembered pleasures was going with the family to the "forks of the crick." Every fall, money came in from the crops, and we all loaded into a surrey or wagon and went down to this tiny little village near the railroad. Dad would take his horses to be shoed, and we would go into the country store that stocked more things than our little store. That's where Mother would buy bolts of cloth to make garments as well as a whole year's supply of things—thread, ribbons, table things, salt, sugar, things like that. The owners of the store had two girls about the age of Frieda and me, and we would play all day at their home on their wide lawn. We ran and jumped and lay down all day on this great carpet of green grass. I didn't think about religion at those times. I enjoyed playing with the other children, and I thought life was very good, indeed.

Oh, I do think there were pleasures living on the farm. We had a swing in the back yard, and we'd pump high until we could see the top of the house. Another thing—Dad fashioned a barrel-staved hammock and tied it to a tree and the end of the house. On summer evenings, it was the perfect thing to laze around in after the chores were done. After we had lived there a few years, we started to put in grass and flowers and shrubs around the picket fence, and everything looked so pretty from the front porch. Mother and Dad often sat there while we kids were out in the yard hunting for frogs and feeding them insects. We liked to watch their long tongues come out, scoop up the bugs and snap their mouths shut.

Ours were simple pleasures, like Dad's music. Believe it or not, he had a sense of fun. He showed it most with his musical talent. He had one of those chapel organs—I think he managed to get it for free—and somehow parted with enough money to give all four of us lessons from a neighbor. Frieda was the only one that had talent. Before we left the farm, she was playing ragtime. Anyhow, we'd all stand around the organ while Dad played chords, and we would sing hymns and folksongs. As strict as he was about discipline and routine, there were times when he would call us together in the evening and say, "Leave those dishes and come in here. We're going to sing."

He played several other instruments, too—accordion, harmonica and the Jew's harp. Do you know what a Jew's harp is? You put this metal frame in your mouth. It has a string, and you blow on it and at the same time, you pluck it with your finger. So it's vibrating and you are blowing and plucking at the same time to make the sounds, sort of like a cross between a harmonica and a guitar.

My favorite listening time was when he played the bones. He would take these rib bones from our meat, hogs ribs I think, and put two of them in one hand. Each of them curved away from each other, and as he moved his arm across his chest, he worked those old bones. He clicked them first together slowly in a tapping beat, but gradually his fingers flew and clicked up a frenzy. It was almost unbelievable, the way he could make those bones go as fast as you please!

As we grew older, someone in the neighborhood would give a party, like Aunt Em. She'd have parlor games, and—I blush to think of it now—but she let us do grown up kissing games like Spin the Bottle and Post Office. I sat watching, mostly. I don't think Dad and Mother knew about those parties. Aunt Em was surprisingly open-minded for her time.

Mostly, Frieda and I stuck together—we were only two years apart—and on rainy afternoons we'd say, "Let's go upstairs and write poems." Writing verses came easily to us. In school, we loved the poetry in our McGuffey Readers. My favorites were John Greenleaf Whittier—especially "Snowbound" because we went through something like that, too—and Edgar Allan Poe. Do you like "Annabel Lee"? I think it was my favorite poem at the time. Frieda continued writing verses over many years—I often go back to her poems to recall some of the details of farm life and the simple pleasures we encountered every day. Mine were different, in keeping with our personalities. At first, I chronicled big events like the sinking of the Titanic. Most of those early poems I did are lost because of the disruption in my life, but I've given you a notebook with my writing as I took it up again after I married your father.

One of the greatest joys of my life was going to school. We'd hear all these other kids in the neighborhood say they hated for school to start, and none of us could understand it. I guess it was my insatiable mind that craved an education. Once we got through the McGuffey Readers, we went on to the Ellson series, which introduced us to the classics like *Tale of Two Cities, David Copperfield, Julius Caesar*. We were reading books like that by the eighth grade.

When we were in Garfield, the other three girls had already started in school, and I was allowed to go with them, so I knew my ABCs by the time I was five. When I got to "L," I said, "A lemon—o—pea." My sisters laughed at this, but instead of thinking I was smart or clever, I felt they were making fun of me.

But what got me in trouble was my fiery temper. I took it out on a boy who pulled my hair. I was so angry that I picked up a stick—a piece of barrel hoop—and whapped him around the legs. Well, that was enough for the teacher. She told my parents that she couldn't teach five-year-olds now. So I couldn't go to school until we moved to the farm.

Our school was one of those one-room schoolhouses you've probably heard so much about. There were about twenty of us in grades one through eight. The older ones taught the younger ones. And we had to go to the front and sit on benches to recite our lessons. Our subjects were the usual ones—language, math and history. But we also studied agriculture, hygiene, anatomy, physiology and circulation of the blood, all that was known about science at the time. I loved algebra and especially grammar. Grammar, grammar, grammar! We diagrammed, we parsed, we wrote. One day I did slip up in a paper I wrote on the care of the teeth. I said that candy was "liable to break the teeth," but the teacher faulted me for that and wrote on my paper, "*likely* to break the teeth." People downgrade the country schools, but I think for being as isolated as we were that we got a fairly decent basic education.

I don't have any memory of sadistic teachers. Oh, if the kids whispered too much, they got the hickory stick. Mostly, we would have to stand on the floor in front of the class. We'd be too ashamed to do that, so we didn't get into trouble like some of the others. I do remember one insensitive teacher. He didn't let me move away from the door in winter, and my feet froze. He allowed most of the kids to move next to the Burnside stove except those in the back of the room where I was. My heels had scabs and pus for days after that. I think I told you that Mother was generally submissive, but she stood up against that. I can't imagine her jumping on anyone, but she did go up to the school and wrote on the blackboard her disapproval of the way he had treated me.

You asked about the seasons. In the fall, we had leaf turning, not as brilliant as in New England, but beautiful. Winters were chilly, with some snow, an occasional blizzard. We nearly froze in our bedroom upstairs! It was hard to get out from under the covers on those mornings. So Mother promised pennies to the first one downstairs and dressed. You might know it was little Laura who won the contest. I seemed to go for those things.

Now in the summers, there was quite a lot of lightning. You didn't see any house without a lightning rod. Whenever there came up a storm, you had to go out and disconnect the telephone line or the lightning would come into your house, so you ran out the minute you knew the storm was headed your way. You left the line hanging, you see, so it would go into the ground. Once I was standing in the doorway when the line was disconnected, and the lightning struck close enough that, I'm telling you, the sound of it nearly shattered my eardrum! Dad was leery of these storms and I don't blame him. Everybody had a cellar, but not under the house. It was what we called a smokehouse, and the cellar was dug under that. During a storm, he gathered the whole family and took us down to the cellar until it was over.

You should see the night sky there sometime. Oh, it was a blinking picture of stars. Not a cloud, just inky black with millions of little white dots! At night, in the summer time, you could locate the big dipper and all those different star groups. We were lucky—often we got a glimpse of the aurora borealis. It's a lovely, shimmery thing, like fading rainbows dancing. And we saw Halley's Comet. That was in 1910. We stood out in the back yard, and oh, it was as clear as could be and we could see the long tail. I think Mark Twain wrote something about seeing that, too. It comes every seventy-five or seventy-six years. There was quite a to-do about it in 1986 when it came over again, and my sisters and I corresponded remembering that we were still here when it came around again.

Spring was the best season. That's when you get the most rain, and everything is green and smells so earthy. You get this ecstatic feeling that only comes with spring. I would run through the fields thinking this was the best life ever. That was before religion took over in me, and my happiness turned to fear. You took life as it was in the present moment. You didn't dwell on the drawbacks or inconveniences—you didn't regard them as drudgery. Oh, sometimes thinking too much about the conditions played havoc with your emotions. Because we all knew that things were not as good as they should be, and we sometimes wished they were better. But we mostly threw that off. It seems incredible to me now that there was a time in my life when the only feeling of unhappiness was when spring was gone.

❧❧

So this was the Eden of her youth. Not perfect, as in that great Biblical myth of the first garden, but in her memory as close to idyllic as anything she could have desired. She had reminded me of the time we spent together shelling peas or peeling peaches for canning. These were moments of closeness that I had unconsciously shifted to the depth of my brain, pleasant times with her that I had long since forgotten. That is, until several months after her passing, on a spring day at the high school where I taught.

❧❧

Their assignment was to read Edgar Allan Poe's "The Tell-Tale Heart"—all three of my ninth grade English classes. We were nearing the end of the school year, and I yearned to be sniffing the lilacs outside my classroom window instead of dealing with ninety hormone-driven teen-agers addicted to horror stories.

Lunch break was ending. I swallowed my sandwich nearly whole, grabbed a pair of scissors from my desk, bolted outside and surreptitiously snipped a few scraggly blooms, inhaling their subtle and elegant scent. Scurrying back to my room in time for the last bell, I plopped my bouquet into a pencil can and shoved the writing instruments back into a desk drawer. No time to run for water. As the students trooped in, I mentally blocked out their noisy chatter. The cocked heads of the lilacs drooped a bit, yet their fragrance was transporting me to another time, another place.

❧❧

I am eleven again on an early June day at our home in the desert southwest. We could easily melt in the 95-degree heat, but the air is dry. My mother and I sit in the shade on the east side of our tiny wood-frame house, shelling peas for canning. Near my bedroom window, a huge lilac bush drips purple blooms, sways softly in a delicate breeze and sends its redolent fragrance our way. I sit cross-legged on the grass watching my mother's busy hands. Our task is simple—to snap the peapods open, thumb the peas into a metal pot and discard the shells in a bucket.

While we work, my mother is telling me about her favorite writers. Today it is Poe and she tells me the story of "The Pit and the Pendulum." Snap! The peapod crackles as she describes the knife coming closer! I shudder, visualizing that instrument of torture swimming over the man in the story. She greatly admires Poe's writing.

After we finish the bushel of peas, she gets up from her chair. With a knife used to conquer recalcitrant pods, she slices stems from the lilac bush until she has gathered a purple handful. She carries her makeshift floral arrangement into the house, finds a large water glass to hold it and sets it gently down on the crocheted doily gracing our claw foot oak table. She takes down from a bookshelf a book of Poe's stories and hands it to me.

"Don't read these if they scare you too much," she says.

What stays with me is not the goose-bump terror felt when reading those gripping tales. Later, I will teach the stories to a younger generation jaded by the violence seen in movies and often times directly experienced in their own lives. For the most part, they react phlegmatically to Poe as an early writer of horror stories, but I am from a different era. Poe's descriptions still give me shudders. But what I remember most clearly about that summer day is this: snapping green peas, picking lilacs and talking endlessly about literature with my mother.

☞◦⟨

The bell rang signaling the end of the lunch period. My ninth graders trooped in flirting and giggling but finally settled down to deposit their homework in the fifth period basket. Backpacks stuffed with I-pods, cell phones and laptops rustled as the students slid them under their seats. The noisy hum began to fade, and pages crackled as the students opened their textbooks to Poe's famous story. I began dryly by attempting to elicit their understanding of "sagacity" and "derision." But their interest is in the last sentence of the story—*"Villains!" I shrieked, "Dissemble no more! I admit the deed!—tear up the planks!—Here, here!—it is the beating of his hideous heart!"* Sensing a teaching moment, I assigned a short writing paper asking them to speculate, given the scant evidence in the story, on a possible motive for the crime.

A friendly freshman passing my desk on his way to the pencil sharpener noticed my makeshift flower vase and asked with innocent curiosity, "What's the deal with the flowers?"

I simply could not explain why it's perfect to have a bouquet of lilacs on my desk.

Chapter 6

Innocence Lost

For I had expected always
Some brightness to hold in trust,
Some final Innocence
To save from dust …
            —Sir Stephen Harold Spender
            from "What I Expected Was"

Three things I never understood—why Mother and Dad neglected them and didn't see the risks to us. One was that open well. Another was letting us take matches up the dark staircase to light our way, what with those mattresses full of straw. The third was Ezra Kingston. He was a hobo that traveled the neighborhood. Oftentimes when we played outside, he was there, out in the road. Sometimes he would enter our yard, and once, when I was six or seven, Ezra Kingston lifted me and took me in his arms. The way he looked at me made chill bumps run up and down my spine. He had a reputation. I can't understand why Mother and Dad weren't worried.

We had a close call when I was around ten. Frieda was twelve, and we were doing some grocery shopping for Mother in a small store about two miles away. Ezra Kingston was there staring at us, and Frieda made me look—sure enough, he had a certain grin on his face that made us shudder. We saw him take a rope out of his pocket and wind it around his wrist. While we were finishing up, he apparently decided to take off. Frieda knew all about what he did from our neighbor Mrs. Carraway. She had rescued a little girl who passed by her house crying. The girl's clothes were practically all torn off, and she told Mrs. Carraway that it was Ezra Kingston who did it. We weren't sure how bad this might have been for her, but we didn't want to meet a similar fate.

We left the store and headed home but became aware that he was following us. Frieda told me to run and run fast to the nearest house. That was the home where a shoemaker and his wife lived. We banged on the door and Frieda told him in a shaky voice, "He's following us! He takes little girls into the woods and kills them!" But the shoemaker said, "Oh, Mr. Kingston won't hurt you." It turned out that the shoemaker's wife was the sister of Ezra Kingston. But she saw the fear in our eyes and she took us part of the way home. When she left us, we dodged all the rest of the way hiding in the weeds, terrified of someone stalking us. We told Mother and Dad, but you know, I don't think they took it too seriously. Now, how do you figure that one? They were so protective and Dad wanted to raise us on a farm to keep us from learning about the world, and yet ... .

Now I'm going to tell you something that I hadn't intended to reveal. But since we've been talking so openly, I guess now is the time. It's about my grandfather, your great-grandfather Peter Bowman.

Unfortunately, I didn't luck out in getting a nice grandfather. I should tell it truthfully: He was a lustful, lecherous old goat, now that it can be told. When I was a young teen-ager, during a visit to the "Grandma house," I went outside to the farmyard where my grandfather was working. He startled me by grabbing and starting to fondle me in a frightening way, and I ran terrified back into the house. I was too embarrassed and shy to say anything about it to the aunts, and I doubt if they would have believed me anyway.

You might find this hard to believe, but when I was back there for a reunion with my sisters a few years ago—I think I was about seventy—I shared this story with my sister Irma. And she told me that she had experienced the same thing but also kept silent. I already told you that your Aunt Irma was not at all timid, but she told me she lived in fear of our grandfather. In those days, we did not talk about such things, so it took me all these years to get brave enough to say what really happened.

It was right about this time that I began walking in my sleep—I told you about that, didn't I? I remember it clearly. The strange thing was that I knew what I was doing. I was looking for some papers or pieces of clothing. And they said to me, "What are you looking for?" And I replied, "Oh, I'm looking for these pay—pars." It's the kind of crazy stuff you dream about, but my eyes were wide open, and I think everyone believed that I was awake—how can you be asleep and remember all this? Now why was I the only one in the family that did that? And why do I remember it to this day?

I don't know if the sleepwalking had a connection to the incident with my grandfather, but it was also around the time that I was beginning to let my fears take over, those religious fears. And there were other worries, too. I began to wonder if I was the odd one of the family and if I was being offensive to the others. I wanted to be like Frieda, do everything exactly like she did. Now that's not normal.

Anyway, I was known as the quiet one. In front of the others, I would be dumb. But you know that feeds on itself. I know they noticed it, that I wouldn't do any talking. When they were all chattering and thinking up small talk, I would simply sit, listening but not participating. Because they chattered about things that seemed so unimportant, or not important enough for me to comment on. Now where I got those ideas, I don't know, but I was interested in intellectual things and things that were going on in the world. So I didn't relate to people around me, you see. I wasn't interested in what other people were doing and saying. Frieda did help me with that. She illustrated how you make small talk with people by asking them something about themselves or what they might be interested in. Dumb me, I didn't figure that out until Frieda gave me some instruction. I suppose I thought that everything you say should be brainy and lofty. Yes, my mind did me a lot more harm than good. That was my perfectionism. Here I am now, telling you all these things, things I wouldn't have thought of saying before. I guess I'm making up for lost time, talking here with you.

So that's the way I grew up. I felt isolated, that's all, different from everybody. I didn't want to reveal my inward thoughts or feelings, so I hid them. I did talk some to Frieda, but not as much as I would have liked. Later on after she grew up, it was Emma that I really bonded with. We had all kinds of talks about morality and philosophy and literature, things like that. But for the most part, I was unwilling to release myself, to be who I was for fear of being embarrassed by someone. As I've told you, that was mostly Dad. He would not have understood how his mocking and mimicking affected me, really all of my life.

We did have outside social occasions with friends, parties, and events at school and church, where I did mix and socialize part of the time. I liked to participate in the plays we had. We mounted curtains and all took parts. But that was easy. I could hide behind the words of the script. But face to face with people, I was shy. I know the other girls socialized more than I did. I became known as a bookworm. I found a book once that talked about "uncommunicativeness." It gave an awful picture of people that don't talk and how they turn out. I was sorry I read it after that.

But I was still glad for Frieda and my other sisters, even if I was the oddball of the family. It helped to have them around when Dad smashed the cat around the tree and when we lost our dear dog Teddy. That's Teddy, for Theodore Roosevelt. Teddy was given to Carl before we left Garfield, and we brought him with us in the wagon when we moved to the farm. Dad fixed up a doghouse and let him into the front yard. Teddy would come out, and we swore he was smiling! But there was this family in the community, the Harmstons, and one of the children put out poison on a dead sheep. Teddy found it and ate some of the flesh. Of course, it poisoned him. We were all so broken up about it that Mr. Harmston offered in return to give us a spaniel puppy of theirs. But we missed Teddy badly, and we were so angry with the Harmstons for letting one of their kids do that, so Dad said, no. Later we did get a mongrel pup called Shep, but he foamed about the mouth, and Dad had to shoot him.

When I was a young teen, I began to be somewhat aware of a world beyond our existence there on the farm. I remember the tragedy of the Titanic, which sank in 1912. Dad would go down to the country store every week and pick up the largest newspaper in the state, and he had us reading about things that were happening. I felt so bad for all those people who died that I wrote my first major poem about the sinking of the Titanic. It got published in the local paper, thanks to Dad, who submitted it. We definitely were aware of the outbreak of World War I—oh yes, I remember exactly—I was in the fields picking berries. It was like when Kennedy was shot, you remember exactly where you were—someone from a neighboring farm came running over to our house and cried out, "There's war in Europe!"

There were things closer to home, too, which broke my innocence. I'll tell you about one tragedy that happened out in our community. We knew about this because it took place in the little village where Dad had the country store, right by the railroad, the one he sold when Mother was showing signs of not being able to handle things at home. We did have doctors in the area, usually one country doctor for about fifty families. Our doctor would come to the house, but you can imagine that he couldn't keep up during epidemics like we went through that winter. But there was a young doctor who had taken over a practice of one of our older physicians. Since he was busy getting established, he found room and board with a family with a large house located outside the village. This family had a teen-age daughter about the age of Irma. Her name was Annie. We knew the family because the father ran the railroad office across the railroad tracks from our store. Annie was quite lively, happy and gay, and she became a friend of Irma's. When the crews of the trains went by, she waved. We were taught not to wave, but she was a bit of a flirt.

Well, Dr. Stilton and Annie fell in love, and they asked Annie's family if they could get married. Her mother was adamant that Annie was too young. But they were so in love, and they planned to elope, evidently. One day, the rumors flew all over that Annie's body had been found and that she had been pregnant. But where was the doctor? People tried to find him to give him the awful news. No one could find the doctor. Was he visiting someone who was sick? For some reason, it wasn't thought at first to check his office, but that's where the sheriff finally went and found him dead. He'd taken poison. Apparently, he had performed an abortion on her that went awry. In his suicide note he stated, "I knew where I made the mistake." He could have meant during the operation, perforation happened and she bled to death. Or he could have accidentally given too much morphine for her system. I don't think anyone knew for sure. Annie's mother received letters from all over the United States blaming her for the tragedy, but also some of sympathy. I thought about writing a ballad about Annie and the doctor, but I couldn't bring myself to do that. The story made me too weepy whenever I thought about it.

Life on the farm went on in its routine way, season after season. With each passing year, I began learning that life had its moments of pain and embarrassment and loss. Early on, I fell in the outdoor toilet, and Irma had to fish me out and clean me up. There were no sitting boards, so it wasn't difficult for a little child to have an accident like that. Oh, did my Aunt Lila give Dad a piece of her mind about not fixing it better. On the farm, Carl lifted me by the hair of my head in the corncrib, and Dad didn't punish him. I guess I had provoked Carl in some way. "A boy has to defend himself," Dad told me in his gruffest tone. I didn't take to brothers much after that.

Other disappointments occurred. Some of the other kids—I can't remember which ones—took my only doll, the one given to me by the aunts, and tore its head off ... no, that's too sad to tell. And I got lice—I was the only one in the family—and had to have my head washed with some awful red stuff to get rid of them. I had picked them up from school—it seemed that I was the runt of bad occurrences. My head itched horribly, and Frieda checked and found these nests of lice—ugh, I shudder now to think about it. Mother got this solution—you can't use that now—it's too dangerous, bleaches the skin—but it did cure it right up. Also, I lost some of my six-year molars before we could get through to Dad about the importance of regular dental care. This dentist—he had a little foot machine—oh, did it hurt when he drilled. He didn't have the modern equipment, and they didn't give numbing medicine at that time.

But nothing could compare to the winter when all of us got sick. That was in 1908 soon after I had turned nine. Margaret was a year old, and Emma hadn't been born. Our brother Tommy was four. Dad was ecstatic to have finally a couple of sons amidst all those girls. And Tommy was a real delight. He was what you might call precocious. He talked early and said the cutest things. Before he was around three, he talked as clearly as an adult, "The other day Gretchen was bothering me, so I slapped her good for it!" Now where he got that, I don't know because we weren't allowed to fight, and neither Mother nor Dad ever struck us. Some kids are like that—born smart. But Tommy was accident prone, too. When he was around a year old, he swallowed Gretchen's ring and was choking, turning blue. Gretchen ran out into the fields and called Dad, "The baby's choking!" Dad came running as fast his heavy self would let him. His lips were white, but he grabbed Tommy by the heels and thumped him hard on the back. Well, that ring came flying out! The little tyke wasn't so fortunate a year later when he fell out of bed and broke his arm. Dad was a mile away at church ringing the bell—he took pride in doing that every Sunday—and the rest of us hadn't left yet to attend the service. Mother told us to run as fast as we could to tell Dad that Tommy's arm was broken. The bone stuck clear through the flesh. I don't know whether Dad put it back himself or we got the doctor or what, and whether they set it or put it in a splint. I was so scared that I can't recall exactly what was done. But I do know that for the rest of his short life, for the next two years, Tommy's couldn't use that arm very well. While he was recuperating, Mother would rock him and sing him one of the folk songs that she learned from her uncle. He caught on fast and would hum along with her.

The sickness that winter started with whooping cough, then measles, then tonsillitis, then mumps. Every one of us caught them, each and every disease, one after another, except Mother and Dad. I suppose they had some immunity from their own childhood. People expected you to have those diseases, you see. There were no shots. Whooping cough was the worst—we were terribly sick. You would draw in your breath and whoop and strangle and throw up. We ran out of rags and finally had to use papers to catch the vomit. I remember soliciting papers from the neighbors to help out, before I got sick. With so many of us, we each re-infected the others. I don't know how Mother and Dad held up, especially Mother. She was nursing Margaret at the time. I remember her taking naps during the daytime. She would snooze, but she and Dad were up thirty nights straight that winter. Aunt Em came over when she could, but she had her own family to attend to. Carla got pneumonia on top of the whooping cough, and I remember her crying with a towel wrapped around her head to help her headache. That's what got Tommy—the pneumonia.

Carla and Irma realized what was happening to our little brother before Frieda and I did. Tommy had been sleeping in a room off the living room, and Dad came to us and said, "Did you know our dear little Tommy boy died last night?" Frieda went to pieces. I probably should have grieved, but I didn't feel it quite as much.

Our grief over losing Tommy was not communal. We had our own ways of dealing with loss according to our personalities. For me, the less I expressed myself the better, since any show of emotion would reveal me as weak. Frieda by nature was fairly emotional, and Mother was weeping to herself most of the time. And Dad—I saw him cry only twice—and this was one of those times. He lay down on Mother's bed in the living room and broke down sobbing while Mother stroked his head.

We set up Tommy's casket in the living room. He was dressed in a shroud.

Aunt Em brought us all in and asked us to kiss him goodbye. She meant well, and I loved Tommy, but it seemed creepy to me all the same. In Garfield before I was five, a little girl had died. The other three girls went to the funeral. I didn't want to go, but had to do it anyway. She had a doll in her arms. It made me so sad. But this was worse—I had to make myself lean down and kiss Tommy's cold, cold lips. Ever since, I haven't wanted to view a corpse. If I do go to a memorial service, I do it out of respect for the survivors. I want to remember people as I have known them in their daily lives.

Chapter 7

After the Madness: Masks

The play is done—the curtain drops,
Slow falling to the prompter's bell;
A moment yet the actor stops,
And looks around, to say farewell.
It is an irksome word and task:
And when he's laughed and said his say,
He shows, as he removes the mask,
A face that's anything but gay.
            —William Makepeace Thackeray (1811-1863)

A cousin who was working in the mental health field obtained copies of our grandmother's state mental hospital records. Following are relevant excerpts.

From: Abstract of History, Norton State Mental Hospital
Esther Bowman Delaney, patient
Dec. 22, 1925

Family History: Patient's parents are both dead. Neither parent was ever insane, epileptic, mental defective, criminal, pauper, alcoholic, or drug addict. Neither parent ever had syphilis, tuberculosis, or any other severe constitutional disease. Committing physicians state that one sister and one uncle have been insane.

Personal History: Patient is married and has (given birth to) nine children, all said to be normal. Committing physicians state that patient has previously been in the State Hospital (Sept.

1916) and was discharged Jan., 1923. They state that patient did not suffer from convulsions or chorea during childhood; that she has never had syphilis; has never been addicted to the use of alcohol or drugs; has never been guilty of a misdemeanor or other crime; has never had a surgical operation; has had no acute infectious diseases. Previous to present illness, patient was said to have been peaceful, honest, and truthful.

Present Illness: First symptoms of present illness began about four months ago. Patient talked continuously; was excited and delusional. Patient was said to have had hallucinations. There was a former attack in 1916. Committing physicians state further that she is oriented and that there are lucid intervals.

Diagnosis: Involutional Psychosis
Allen Wentfield, M.D.

Nov. 1, 1932
Physical condition normal. Mentally, patient is mildly disturbed.

April 18, 1950
There had been no noticeable change in this patient's condition. She has been a constant complainer. Several days ago because of back and hip complaints an X-ray was taken to rule out possible fracture ... The findings were negative ... She was considerably overweight. She has been reported to eat everything she can get hold of. Age 80. This A.M. at 8:30 she expired suddenly. Mrs. Harkin, the ward attendant was present at her bedside. Her family in Norton was notified ... Mental diagnosis when admitted to this hospital Involutional Melancholia.

Mary Demarist, M.D.

❧

Another interesting find produced at the cousins' reunion in 1992 was a newspaper clipping of my grandparents' celebration of their fiftieth wedding anniversary. I presented this clipping during one of our later interviews, thinking that Mother would be pleased to know there was an actual written record. Instead, she was stunned. Nearly fifty years had passed, yet she claimed to have no knowledge that this event took place. No one had bothered to tell her. Perhaps for the rest of the family, she remained, as she had growing up, invisible, odd, and finally, the one who left.

Item in *The Norton Daily News*, Sept. 29, 1942

Of interest here is the recent celebration of the golden wedding anniversary of Mr. and Mrs. Henry M. Delaney of Norton, which was marked by a family dinner party at the Silver restaurant on Sept. 26.

The couple was united in marriage Sept. 25, 1892, in the Bountiful Community Church near Garfield, PA. In 1917 Mr. Delaney received employment at the Norton State Hospital. A number of years ago Mr. Delaney was retired. Their family consists of seven daughters who served as schoolteachers previous to their marriages, and one son. All were educated at Norton High; and one daughter, Mrs. Irma Delaney Thomas is employed as a teacher here.

Mrs. Laura Delaney Johnson of Albuquerque, NM, a daughter, was unable to be present for the celebration.

So right after Mother tried to do away with herself, Irma took charge of the family. Once Mother got rescued, Irma gave us all jobs. Boil water, get clean clothes, that sort of thing. She kept us busy so that we could deal with our shock and horror. In an instant, she became the mother of the family. I don't know how we all would have gotten through the next few years without her. She was a natural leader, a take-charge kind of person. But she and Dad had their go-rounds and clashed a lot. I guess they were too much alike. She would stand up to him, but as I mentioned before, I was too timid to consider doing that.

But one thing we all praise him for. My dad—that man, in order to keep all of us children in school, made arrangements for us to live that next school year in Littlefield. It was the closest small town, about four miles away from the farm. We stayed there that winter in a rented apartment above a store. Irma was teaching already—you could do that after the eighth grade if you passed the state examination—but Frieda and I were already attending high school there. The rest of the kids were in grade school, and he didn't want to break up a school year. So in the spring he rented a freight car on the railroad, loaded our furniture in it, and once the school term ended, he took us all to Norton so that we could be near Mother.

You might be wondering who took care of the farm. I think we deserted it until he got it sold. It was after we had been in Norton for a while. I guess he used the rest of that summer to sell the animals and crops and things like that. He didn't bring the rest of us into the—what you might call business parts of it. But as I look back, I see there was some value there. I know we had milk cows but we had only a sparse number of crops growing at that time—corn, wheat. He must have harvested those, but I really can't recall what might have happened. We had 108 acres, but most of it was hilly. There were few tillable parts, but we had sheep because they can live on the hillsides. And I suppose he may have stashed away some money from the sale of the store two or three years before, when he saw signs that she was getting ... she was beginning to show those symptoms. Anyway, I think that's when he sold it. I don't know for sure, but that must have been what we lived on for a short while, at least, for the next year when we lived in Littlefield.

Once we got to Norton the following year, Dad rented a house. The following year, he moved us to a house that he bought. It had a bathtub and indoor plumbing, and oh, were they luxuries! And we had gas to cook with. No more chopping wood and shoveling coal. So some things got easier for us. Frieda and

I were in high school, but Irma stayed out for a while to get the four younger ones settled. After a time, we all fell into a routine. There was not as much work, but we each took on a role. I still baked bread because the other girls had avoided learning how to do it. I'd set the starter at night, and before leaving for high school, I'd put the dough to rise. To keep it warm, I'd wrap it in blankets and bake it after school let out. Irma finally resumed her education, going with us to Norton High. She had to double up on courses, and the three of us ended up graduating the same year. We sewed up identical "middy" dresses and had our graduation picture taken together. I guess that you could call that a triumph considering what we'd been through.

So we were right there in the same town where Mother lived in the hospital. When I think of the terrible turn in Mother's life, I have to say that I was so happy that there was this place of refuge for her. She had good physical care and an absence of responsibility. She had friends at the hospital. She had freedom to go and come as she pleased and often took walks with us on the pleasant hospital grounds. Dad was allowed to take her home for the day whenever he wanted to, which was frequently, and he would take her back to the hospital at night.

Anyhow, she got to the point where she was ... she got so much better that we could bring her home occasionally for visits. They had her in what was called the open ward. It was kind of like a nice apartment. I know, you've heard horror stories, about mistreatment of mental patients in these institutions. There was one in *Time Magazine* in the 1940s that worried me so, something about mental patients being herded into too little space and being treated like animals. And I do recall now that my sister Margaret told me that she once saw Mother with a black eye. But I can't believe it was from abuse. She could have fallen down or something. Besides, Dad would have been right on that, if it really happened.

The hospital building was solid gray stone, and the lawn was so enormous that it served as the park of the town. Concerts and lectures were held there on the weekends. That's where I first came in contact with Chautauqua. This was the traveling Chautauqua, and they would pitch the tents right on the hospital grounds. For the first time in my life, I could hear lectures on current happenings, and I began to get my eyes open to the wider world. So in some ways, it was better to be in Norton than isolated on the farm. We got introduced to cultural things that had not been available to us earlier.

And shade, oh, I can still remember the benches to sit on, and the townspeople would stroll along on those grassy grounds and not be mindful that this lovely stone building housed mental patients. It was a pleasant place to be, and I guess we didn't think about what might be going on for the people inside those walls. Because Mother had these privileges, and we could take her out any time we wanted to, walk around, or sit together on the lawn in summer. She seemed to improve over time, and Dad was told he could take her home on Sundays to visit with us as long as he took her back.

But I wouldn't want you to think that life was not without its sorrowful moments. Here's something that gives me a lump in my throat. Your cousin Lois, who was Margaret's daughter, told about visiting your grandmother, and she told me she remembers Mother weeping, saying over and over, "I failed the family, I failed the family." And Lois would say, "No, you didn't, but how do I get this over to you?" Even now, I feel like crying when I remember these things.

We would do up picnic baskets for her and take them down to the hospital. I remember cooking an entire meal—usually, it was fried chicken and potatoes and cabbage salad—and taking it down to her to relieve the hospital staff. It seemed as if it fell to me to do all those things for Mother—bringing down the Sunday dinner to her—I guess the others knew I would do it. I suppose they cared, but they knew I would do it. I'm the one who had to break the news to Mother that her mother had died—right there in her own bed in the "Grandma house." And she asked, "Why didn't you tell me?" And I had to reply more than once, "I'm telling you now!" As to whether it was a sorrowful thing for her, I doubt it. She couldn't feel much pain for anyone else because she was so centered on herself.

High school graduation 1918
Seated: Irma (L) and Laura (R). Standing: Frieda

I think I mentioned that Dad got a job at the hospital. He hadn't worked for the entire year we were in Littlefield because he was busy getting things moved to Norton. But he made friends with the most important people—he was so gregarious—and he got acquainted with a woman whose husband was there, and she wanted to hire a private attendant. Dad never knew a stranger and met her through visiting with some of the staff, so he knew quite a bit about a number of the patients. The regular attendants were paid extremely low wages, about thirty dollars a month. But this woman paid my dad nicely to take care of this man, about twice the amount that he would have gotten if he had a whole ward to take care of. That's the way he supported us until we all got through school. It was a given that Irma and Frieda and I would pitch in to help the younger children.

After the man died, Dad got a regular attendant's job, which paid a little better by that time. Of course, Dad was getting well acquainted with the superintendent of the hospital. Why they got to be buddy-buddy! I honestly think Henry Michael Delaney could get to be friends with the President if the President were around! Apparently, he would go to the superintendent's office, and they would talk up a storm.

This was around the time when Mother came into her money, and the superintendent recommended a psychiatrist. You see, all her living expenses were paid for since it was a state institution, but that didn't include private care or counseling. So Dad took Mother to this psychiatrist for about a year. And she improved enough to come home for good—I think this was after about seven years—and live with the rest of us. For a while, she was normal as could be. But later she had to go back because she couldn't face the problems.

When she did come home, there were some other changes in her. For instance, she took over her own money affairs. She had always taken Dad's advice, but earlier Dad had become her guardian. While in the hospital, she couldn't sign any papers or anything, but for the time she was with us those three years, she functioned well. And another thing, the psychiatrist advised Dad, don't watch her. You see, when we took her home, she knew that all the time somebody was with her, that we were watching to see that she didn't attempt suicide again. That was the understanding among us, as I told you earlier. Nobody left her alone. But the therapist said, don't do it. He could see how that would weigh on somebody's mind if they knew they were being watched all the time. But he still wanted her to take some kind of control over her life.

The psychiatrist also advised Dad to let her take charge of herself. She had always asked Dad's opinions, and she continued to do that. But when he got too domineering, she did show some independence. Once she got brave enough to tell him something that had bothered her for a long time. He had a habit of folding his hands together over his great huge waist and drumming his fingers on that huge belly of his. This happened when he was satisfied, or when he was telling her what she should do or not do. And she asked Dad if he would stop doing that. I don't recall if he ceased, but I'm sure he was really shocked—throughout their marriage, she had been so meek and submissive.

So she was home for about three years. She was there when I went away to nursing school. But when she had to go back, they didn't tell me. I guess they thought I'd worry—but why should I worry? I cared, but I was starting my own life. And I think I should have been told that she had to go back. It wasn't the only time that I was excluded from the family. No wonder I came to think of myself as pretty weird.

As for Mother, though, she had started to fret and do the "worry talk," so that was the signal that she would have to return to the hospital. But she was not insane, I'll never believe that. A friend of mine in later years, one of the few who knew this story, told me, "Your mother was not insane. She just retired from life." And that's the best diagnosis I've ever heard.

During those few years at home, I imagine that it was so strange for her. You see, when she ended up in the mental hospital, the younger girls were little kids, not teen-agers. Carl was slightly younger than me, so he was in high school by the time we graduated. But now she was away from us most of the time. And things on a farm, you know, are so much different from things in town. And as I look back, I can see why she couldn't take the pressures and problems of everyday life. She came home to two teen-agers, Margaret and Emma, who probably sassed her some. We older ones didn't dare to open our mouths to Mother and Dad because if we did, why, Dad jumped down our throats. But now, in this new and unfamiliar world, she would try to tell the two younger girls how to do things. But kids after they've been liberated don't react like that. As for Mother, I suppose she kept it inside, when the girls talked back. I'm sure she minded it. It distressed her that she couldn't tell them to do something and it would be done, like she did on the farm.

There was another thing, too. The job that Dad had taken with the hospital—it was as a night orderly. So Mother worried terribly about his being away overnight. I maintained that she might have been home longer if he had been sensitive to her needs. I felt he was kind of copping out. Probably he felt with the burdens that he had, that he deserved this, slipping away from the cares of everyday life. But his being away had the same feeling as when we were living on the farm when he stayed away at the store during the week and came home on weekends. I felt strongly that Mother could have coped better and might have made it if Dad had been home at night. Oh, I felt for her so! If he had only realized ... men apparently don't understand those feelings, when they have such a strong sense of self like he did. They can't envision someone who isn't self-sufficient enough.

But as for those religious fears of hers, they disappeared. Really, I heard not a peep about them after she came home. What she did do was worry, worry, worry. She complained that she couldn't stand all the noise around her, the rattle of the dishes, things like that. But I suppose the main thing was security. She was out into a world she wasn't used to. She'd been nowhere else but a farm. She married Dad from her father's farm, and she lived on a farm all while raising us. And with the rest of the family being transported to the town scene and her two babies grown up into adolescents—well, she just couldn't cope.

What I see now is that we had two families. We older girls experienced the hard work but also the pleasures of farm life—the ones I told you about. Carl was a kind of bridge. He experienced some of the farm life, but Dad refused to let him do much of the work. So he wasn't as affected by Mother's leaving as we were, since we took up all the duties that Mother had once done. But after the tragedy, we drew this protective cocoon around the younger girls to shield them from the trauma of it all. At least I thought we did. As I found out later, you can't escape this kind of catastrophe where you lose but don't lose your mother. It has consequences, and we all paid for it in our separate ways.

I think I mentioned that we really owe a lot to Irma. All of us worked together, we really did. But I didn't realize until I was much older, as I look back on it, what responsibility she took for the rest of the family when this happened. I don't think I could offer enough praise for her, for what she did for us. Oh, yes, she was pig-headed and contrary and ornery, really Irish like Dad. She acted out as the clown while we lived on the farm by cutting up and making us laugh. But she told me later, when we corresponded in recent years, that she acted out to cover up. She wrote, "I decided to act the fool to hide my feelings because things were so terrible." She so resented the circumstances and conditions in which we had to live.

It was her nature to be non-conventional, a real rebel. After I had left home, I heard that she took up cigarettes and smoked like a chimney. And once she was married, she did things like sending out her laundry to a lady of the night, who apparently had other pursuits besides being a washerwoman. It would have been unthinkable in our moralistic family to allow someone with a reputation like that to do our laundry! But Irma chose to do the opposite of what she had been taught was proper. I think some of it was for effect. She had that ability to know what she wanted to say. She said it, and you would do it. And you didn't resent her telling you that. So in Norton, she divided up the ironing and the washing and the cooking, and it seems to have gone smoothly.

But along with that sense of obligation she had for the family, she ended up with a volcano of anger that really seethed in her—

this was her resentment against Dad. I guess these feelings built up over lots of years. I think of her as an early feminist type, too, because she may have sensed that she had a lot on the ball but wasn't handed any breaks. But the biggest thing for her was that she never forgave Dad. She told me once, "If he had just once said, 'I appreciate your taking care of my three children,' it would have canceled all that resentment." If he had ever given her a compliment or thanked her, it might have gone a long way. But as you can guess, he wasn't the type to do that.

Irma started teaching in Norton after the three of us graduated from Norton High. We all made such good grades there in high school, and the superintendents knew us, so when Irma applied for a school, it was a foregone conclusion that he would give her a teaching position. Isn't it amazing that you could start teaching after graduating high school? And with Carla and Irma earlier, in those farm areas, you could teach after the eighth grade, which is what they both did. Things changed, and later additional education was required, but it's a good thing we older ones could get jobs, because there were Gretchen, Margaret and Emma—and who would take care of them when the rest of us went off to teach? What would have happened to those three little kids? So she lived at home and took care of them.

Irma wrote to me during recent years that this was the reason she didn't get married right away. That came later, with Harmon. But did I ever tell you about her prior love affair? She fell for this classmate of ours from Littlefield. He dated her and he used to come up to Norton regularly to visit her. Eventually, they became engaged. But finally she told him she had to stay home and take care of the younger girls. He had given her this ring, a lovely ruby. She sold it to me after they broke up. I was so proud of it because I loved anything red—especially rubies. I'll tell you what happened to it in greater detail later. It's a sad thing.

As for me, you remember that Dad took me with him, me alone, when we made those trips to see Mother that winter in Littlefield before moving to Norton. I wondered but didn't question. He moved everyone else to Norton in the summer, except for me. He had arranged temporary lodging for himself at a boarding house in Norton, where he lived while he was getting Mother settled. In order to exchange for board and room, he "offered" my services to the woman—she was taking in roomers trying to support an alcoholic husband—so I fixed meals, changed beds, cleaned rooms. I never thought about rebelling or protesting. For one thing, you wouldn't dare, with Dad. I had to accept it. But I did miss all the excitement of loading the railroad car and moving with the family. Now why was I the one that Dad chose to exclude from the moving preparations? You asked about that. For one thing, I know he could see that my eyes were in heaven, not on earth, and I suppose he thought I wouldn't be any help. He never gave me credit for all the household chores I did around the farm—or maybe he was trying to shake me loose from my religious obsessions.

Yes, my head was in the sky—I was addicted—yes, that's the word—to religion. I continued to feel like I wasn't saved, and I worried about myself nearly all the time. But I have wondered in later years if Dad might have been concerned that I might have suicidal tendencies, like Mother. He tried to keep me from going to church too much in Norton. You can't blame him.

We all continued to live at home, but just as before, I didn't meld with the other girls. I was different, that's all. Oh, we loved each other, and we got along all right, but I think they assumed I would do all the picnic preparations for Mother each week, and that I didn't want to be with them when they went out adventuring.

By this time, Gretchen was out of school and teaching, too. One summer the three of them—Irma, Frieda and Gretchen— left Norton to go to one of the state universities, which was in a town to the east of where we lived. They went to take some summer teaching courses, but they didn't invite me to go along. I suppose I could have spoken up, but, you see, I didn't ever express my feelings out loud—it was part of my problem. So I told them later that I really wanted to stay home and sew for the younger kids. I was so hurt, but I buried it all and did not bring up the subject. On another occasion, they went to the University of Michigan to some kind of teacher's conference on the train, again without me. When they returned, they commented on how dumpy we all looked compared to the women they met at the conference. They had found out how little up-to-date they were. This was in the early 1920s, and clothing and shoe styles were changing. Can you imagine, they went there with high top shoes? Some of the boys teased them when they talked about hoeing corn. "Oh, we *cultivate* corn—why don't you go back to the farm where they hoe corn!" Once I heard that, I was glad I hadn't gone along. Who wants to be embarrassed and thought of as a "hick"?

After we graduated, I got different teaching jobs. One was a district that had coal money, and the pay was so much higher than in Norton itself. I got $125 a month, a nice salary. The money enabled me to help out the younger kids with some of the expenses. Gretchen had gotten through high school by this time and had started teaching, so I tried to make life easier for Margaret and Emma, making sure that they had decent clothes for school and all. During that summer vacation, I bought bolts of cloth and made dresses for them.

When I think about those years, I realize that we covered up the situation with Mother—to ourselves and certainly to our friends. Irma missed out on marrying her first love while Frieda, Gretchen and I—all three of us—experienced break-ups at different times with boyfriends once they learned that Mother was kept in an asylum. You couldn't live in or come from Norton without someone suspecting. When Irma finally did marry, she put on a merry mask of happiness. But I knew that all her jollity was a mask to hide her true feelings.

I realize we all covered up and found ways to cope. Frieda wrote funny poems about living on the farm. But deep down, I know she suffered. One day in high school class, she broke out weeping. When I asked why, she lied. She said that Irma had punched her. I knew that wasn't true because that happened all the time, and Frieda punched back. But finally, she confessed. She had gone to spend a night with a friend, and the mother was kind, not frazzled and worrying all the time like our mother, and the atmosphere there was calm and quiet. "And when I thought about going back home, I cried." We convinced ourselves that we all loved each other, and that was enough. That's how we got through it.

Meanwhile, I was trying to decide what to do with my life. By now I was around twenty-five, not married and didn't have prospects. I liked some of the things about teaching, but the nervous strain was too much for me. I don't think I was cut out for it. I expected my students to love literature and poetry as much as I did. But I couldn't get it over to them. Once I was teaching an essay that told about how a little girl melted into the city strife like a snowdrop in the ocean. I asked them, "What does that mean?" And one of the students, eager to show off, raised his hand and responded, "She melted into the city and the city fell into the ocean."

That was bad enough, but nothing like the day I found a note on the floor once, where a student had dropped it. Thinking back, I wondered if she did it purposely. I had the class writing poems, and she beamed up at me like she was lapping this all up. I picked up the note, which read something like, "There she sits atop her stool. With her greasy specs, she looks like a fool." Oh, was I crushed! But it was a good thing because I came to terms with the fact that teaching wasn't a really good fit for me.

Secretly, I had wanted to go to nursing school after high school, but once I let that out and told Dad, he wouldn't let me. He wanted me to do what the other girls had done, teach school. And all the while, the requirements were increasing, so I used some of those summers between teaching years to pick up courses toward a two-year degree at Grandview Normal School. These were the former teacher's colleges. I was thrilled with college where I got introduced to the poets and writers I still love. I took psychology and history and found the science courses a breeze. Another eye opener to the world out there!

At this point, I got it in my head—which was still stuffed with religion—that I wanted to become a medical missionary. So, on my own, I wrote to the Board of Foreign Missions of the Methodist Church telling them of my hopes and dreams.

I received an answer telling me that I might consider looking at Yale University School of Nursing to obtain the necessary nurse's training because of a new program there that would admit students with only two years of post-secondary education. I wasn't sure about it, so I told Frieda, and if you can believe this, she said, "Where's Yale?" She didn't know, either! That's how provincial we all were. But I did write and got a letter back asking for my transcripts. Based on my high school and teacher's college performance—I guess you wouldn't feel I was bragging too much if I told you I got all A's in high school and that I placed second in a class of fifty at Grandview Normal School—the dean wrote back immediately and offered me a full scholarship including tuition, room and board.

It was hard to convince the family of my decision to accept, but at age twenty-six, I was ready to make up my own mind. Frieda seemed genuinely astonished and asked me over and over, "Why? Why?"

I answered her like this: "If you do what both your mind and heart agree on, well then, it's right. Your mind might agree on doing something but if it isn't what you like in your heart, it won't work. But when your mind and heart go for the same object and have the same direction, you have to go for it." That's what I told her, that my mind and heart want one thing. And I made plans for the first time in my life to leave the family.

Emma circa 1936

Chapter 8

Madness Returned: Emma

When they're laughing at you, when they love you so,
when they hate to lose you, that's the time to go.
                    —Found in Emma Delaney's *"Bits and Pieces,"*
            a little book of philosophic writings.

E mma, our youngest, was a brain, a real intellectual. She sailed through high school with all kinds of honors. She won essay writing contests and the state Latin award. She was popular and pretty—tall and lanky like Dad in his younger years, and she had this gorgeous wavy dark hair. We all thought of her as our family star. All of us had gotten good grades, but we were all especially proud of Emma.

I've often thought about—you know what happened to her later—how much she might have been affected by that terrible day with Mother and the well. But she was only six, and I think she and other little ones slept through it all. I guess we'll never really know, but as I told you, we all gathered round the little ones and tried to protect them from our family tragedy.

Fortunately, Emma's personality was not like Mother's. She had quite a bit of self-assurance—she was no shrinking violet. She was the only of one of us that went straight to college after high school. Dad tried to undermine that and insist that she go right into teaching. But she really wanted to go to college badly and begged him so. At that point, I stepped in and insisted that he should think about this. I confronted him, I'll bet for the first time in my life. But this thing for Emma was extremely important. I told him he ought to let her go because he had this money of Mother's, and he could afford it, and also that she would need it. We didn't have to have a four-year degree at the time to be able to support ourselves. We could pick up courses while we taught. But she needed to be a college graduate. Requirements had changed so much by that time. The state was finally getting its educational legs. Dad did relent and agreed to pay the tuition. And I sent her ten dollars a month for spending money during those years. I think I was the only one who did that—not to brag or anything. Emma and I were close, and the others were caught up in their own lives.

So she applied and got accepted at this church-related college, not a state supported institution. She starred academically, as expected. She majored in English literature and later taught in high school. Anyway, it was in college that she got so interested in philosophy and questions of morality. She was preoccupied with doing the right thing morally. That was some of Dad's influence, too. She had been exposed to religion, and was with us when we joined the Methodist church in Norton. They sprinkled you there, and she wanted to be baptized by immersion. The Methodist church did not have a baptistery, and I can remember taking her to the Baptist church in Norton to be immersed. But she did not harbor the religious fears that I did.

However, she did have all these—what would you call them— inhibitions, I guess. She told me about a psychology class she took, where the professor gave a questionnaire for the students to determine, on some kind of scale, the amount of inhibitions they held. And she, apparently, had the most and the deepest of all in the class. She told me this with a sense of pride. I think she wore them, these inhibitions, like a badge of honor, but the truth was that she couldn't free herself from them. Now I told you that she had an air for self-confidence, but I often wonder if that was a mask. I think she may have projected to others someone she really wasn't. I'm now inclined to think she suffered from low self-esteem, that the "real" Emma was not the one we saw on the outside. As for the inhibitions, I think she had an awful lot of conflict with herself ... but I'm getting ahead of the story.

She was so excited about getting ready for college. Now Margaret and she were the two youngest, but you couldn't find two other people with such opposite personalities. They went through high school together, one class apart. Margaret was a social butterfly. Emma had friends, too, although she lived in Margaret's shadow, being one year younger. Emma told me that Margaret also got the idea that she might like to go to college, too. During the time when the arrangements were being made, Margaret asked her if she could go also, with her. And Emma told her emphatically, "No!" She wanted to be on her own. I understood that because, as I told you, I took my own steps toward independence from the family.

While in college, she met this boy. They seemed a perfect fit for each other, and they went together practically the whole time she was in college. It was understood that they planned to get married. The kids called them Mom and Pop because they were together so much. His name was George. No doubt, he was the one she should have married.

I've told you about how I came out to the Southwest a year after graduating from nursing school, and that's where I met and married your father. But I was concerned about this relationship of Emma's. George had tuberculosis in his family and had broken down with it himself. I was seeing some of these World War I veterans who contracted TB and moved to a dry, warm climate, and they would marry nurses or someone to take care of them. And these girls were left with nothing in their lives but a sick husband. I guess I got carried away with this notion, and I wrote to Carl to ask him to get other dates for her if he could. Now, if I could take it all back, I wouldn't have meddled. I guess that was one of the prices we paid for Mother's illness—we felt so protective and all. I really unburdened myself in that letter to Carl. I don't know what he thought about it all, but I do know that he talked it over with her.

Emma finished her schooling the year after your father and I got married. And I got the idea of writing her and telling her that I'd like to see her get out of "them thar hills." She and I were so much alike. Just like me, she wanted to get out in the world a little bit and see what it was like. Your father had a number of siblings, too, and each sister or brother helped the younger ones, so he understood this, and he was all for it. So I invited Emma to come out and stay with us until she could get settled. I still have regrets about suggesting this. Things might have turned out differently.

She indicated a willingness to take us up on the offer, but she wanted to take her time thinking it over, so she taught a couple years back home after graduating. Meanwhile, she and George broke off their plans to have a wedding. Whether my letter to Carl had any effect, or whether she decided on her own not to marry George, I'm not entirely sure. There were lots of things that Emma didn't share. But after those two years of teaching, she did decide to take us up on our offer, but said she would stay on only if she could find a job. I was shocked later to find out that she and George were still corresponding, and here he was, already married to someone else. I found out, too, that she had written Dad that George was the only one in her life—ever—who knew her faults but loved her anyway. But we all adored and loved her—how could she think that we didn't accept any faults she may have had? I guess I still feel guilty for convincing her to leave the family and come adventuring. I determined never again to interfere with anyone's marriage plans.

She took the plunge and moved out to our area in 1936. She lived with us until she got her first job after she got her teaching credentials established. It wasn't hard for her to get a position. She found one easily in a smaller town on the edge of our city, about ten miles away.

I would have to say that she was really independent-minded and ambitious. One summer she went out to Los Angeles and stayed with one of your father's sisters. She took a course to learn how to be a comptometer operator. You've probably not heard of a comptometer, but it was the forerunner of the desktop calculator. You operated it by keys like a typewriter to get the sums, and it was the coming thing in businesses. She wasn't sure what she wanted to do with her life, and I suppose she was trying out different things. Those were the years when we would travel over to Southern California for vacations to get out of the desert heat, and we would join her and your father's sisters for picnics and trips to the beach. For about two years we had lots of good times.

It was probably a good thing that she found her own place to live because we were too much alike—perfectionists, analytical, systematic. We had trouble living with each other. During the time she stayed with us, she blew up at lots of little things. But I guess I did the same thing—you probably remember my inclination to fly off the handle. I suppose that I hadn't gotten over the fact that Emma was a grown up. And possibly I didn't treat her as an adult, but too much as if I were her mother.

I always felt that Emma had two strikes against her from the start. One was being the youngest in the family. And the other was this perfectionist personality. I do know that she must have gotten told what to do from all sides, since she was the final child. On the farm, for the short while before we moved to Littlefield, we coped with our mother's absence by having a hierarchy of "bosses." As we settled into our new routine in Norton, Irma filled the role of mother for Gretchen, Margaret and Emma. Carl was in his first year of high school, and besides, Dad dealt with him. But I helped out, too, especially with Margaret and Emma. Gretchen was close to high school age and blended into the family and her social groups without too much guidance or direction.

When we moved to Norton, Emma was seven. By the time Mother came home for a while in 1923, she was thirteen. She once told me, "You have no idea after not having a boss for so long, to have a strange woman come into my house and try to boss me." So I guess Emma felt she was handed a new mother, I don't know. And I answered her, "But wasn't it the same?" By that I meant, you see, we older ones bossed the little ones and they didn't seem to mind it. They assumed that we were their parents.

I suppose it was no wonder she had a fixation about being bossed. When your father and I tried to advise her on various things, she would do the opposite. She got tonsillitis frequently and finally was convinced that she needed to have the tonsils removed. I wanted her to come to our home and take care of her after the operation because I'd seen people hemorrhage after a tonsillectomy. But she wouldn't listen to me. Instead, she went to one of her friend's doctors, and he did the surgery right there in his office. Probably gave her chloroform or something. We went right down to this place, and that horse doctor—he took them out right then and there with us as witnesses but didn't even try to get her to a hospital.

During her time in Arizona, she had two love affairs. Naturally, she probably was worried about whether she would ever get married. You worry an awful lot when you get to your mid-twenties. Anyhow, the first one, Sam, was a factory representative for Standard Oil. She really fell hard for him. He was the first guy that interested her since the George thing had ended, but he turned out to be alcoholic and she didn't know it. Once we invited her to come up to our home on a weekend when Sam was in town and made a date with her. I cooperated in every way I could to help her in her romantic life. This one time, I prepared a nice lovely meal. I had bought some wine glasses—I knew that Sam liked to drink—and purchased some wine to serve with the meal. I had to convince your father—he was so against alcohol, much like my Dad. Well, they did accept our invitation to dinner. But Sam didn't arrive at all that evening. Emma found out later that he'd been downtown drinking by himself. So she took to her bedroom crying. Your father was softhearted with her, and he said to me, "She's lucky to know it now—she'll cry more than that if she ever marries that guy. She'd better have her tears now rather than later." He'd been through all of this before, with one of his own sisters. She was married to an alcoholic, so he knew how drink could lead to an early grave.

Emma rarely gave into her feelings in front of anyone, not even me. But this was too much for her. I think that was the start of the thing that broke her. It was a rebound thing, going with the Hispanic fellow. Now Eddie was a high-class young man, mannerly, intelligent and all that. He was also a teacher in another school near where she was teaching. But she felt she had to have someone, I guess, and this was the way she could show Sam that she was having a good time without him. She managed to put on a mask of gaiety to convince everyone around her— including herself—that things were fine.

Now during this time, your father and I were hoping, longing for a baby. We'd been married seven years, and I was going on thirty-eight. Emma knew my longings, and I wondered later on whether she had a fear of being displaced, whether that played into what happened later. I did get pregnant, but had a miscarriage and lost the baby at seven months—it was a little girl. Your father and Emma bought a tiny blue dress and took her body to the funeral home and had a little service for her. They told me all about it, but I wasn't allowed to see the baby or participate in her funeral. They kept women in the hospital for days at that time, you see. I didn't realize it at the time, but I know that I must have resented your father and Emma taking control and not including me. All that grief and anger went inward, down to my soul, just as it had done in my early life.

But miracle of all miracles, I got pregnant with you within the next year, and this time things went better. Meanwhile, Emma seemed to be in good spirits. She was delighted for me, or at least that's what I believed. She was dating Eddie, and they apparently were having lots of fun together. I was so focused on my pregnancy that I didn't notice certain things—that Emma was deceiving all of us.

Only later I discovered that she had purchased a gun, a pistol, through the mail—you could do that—and told me that she often went to a shooting range for target practice. As I told you, she was really independent-minded, and my head was elsewhere at the time. So I didn't ask her about why she was doing it, or even wonder whether she was trying to give me a signal of some kind.

Then came the call. Your father answered.

He looked ashen. He turned to me and said, "Your sister shot herself."

You, my dear daughter, were four months old. The day before this happened, Emma had come over to our place, taken you out to the back yard and rocked and sung to you. I'm sure now that she was saying goodbye.

No words could describe how torn up I was. Eddie came right away and sobbed in my arms. Obviously, he was in love with her. But my first reaction was to get angry—angry with the folks back home who wouldn't believe that it was suicide. I had one outburst over the telephone with Frieda, in which I said, "She's an adult, and if she wants to take her own life, she should have that right!" Frieda wasn't the only one of the family to question how Emma had died. Most of them wanted to believe it was an accident. But Frieda told me she thought that "half breed" had killed her. For a while they even perpetuated the myth that she was murdered. I sent all of Emma's effects back to Dad. Among them was Eddie's fraternity pin. Frieda apologized later, and in time, I think she came to believe the truth that I was telling her.

Emma's "Bits and Pieces" folder was revealing. That's what she called her little book of philosophic writings. When I read through the poems and journal comments, I realized how depressed she was. This poem—"The Fool's Prayer"—when I found it, it made me feel terrible, thinking that I was the King in the poem trying to get the Fool to perform, and the Fool took everything on himself. Or was she thinking I was the fool? Oh, my heart ached when I discovered the writings she had saved! (*See Appendix for some relevant verses of this poem.*) I took all the responsibility for her depression on myself. It struck me that her apparent high sense of self-esteem was a mask covering a deep-seated wound or trauma of some kind. She was so little when Mother had to go away.

The mortician described to us the angle of the bullet wound to the head and had concluded that there was no way it could have been either an accident or a matter of foul play. Clearly, in his mind, she had taken her own life. After the inquest, which corroborated the coroner's conclusions, your father and a friend intervened before the newspaper article came out to make sure the statement was in there in black and white—making sure that it read that Emma had come to her death "not by a criminal act."

Emma earlier had written out a little will, but I hadn't felt that this was connected to some plan to commit suicide. She left her life insurance of $5,000 to me, and I immediately sent the entire amount to Dad along with her effects. There wasn't any way I wanted the family to think I had profited by her death.

And I wrote up a letter to Dad telling of the report from the mortician, and what I knew about Emma's possible motivations. I didn't keep a copy. I don't know whether he shared the contents. Probably not.

As all this was unraveling, I had my own bits and pieces to put together. I was in such a fog but realized that Emma had gone to my doctor not too long before this happened because she said she might get married and she wanted a pre-marital exam. I also recalled that she and Eddie had dated all that school year starting in September—it was now March—and that I had asked her what her plans were for the summer, but she was vague about it. And here's another thing—on her dresser I found a cheap imitation diamond engagement ring. And I think I recall that there was also a cheap wedding ring. I felt like at the time she was trying to tell us something. That if it was found out that she was pregnant—and I strongly suspect that she was—that she wanted us to know that she was engaged or planning to get married. Both rings were lying there with a note. But the note was cryptic, and it could have been interpreted as one of her little philosophical writings. Nevertheless, it showed how hopeless she felt. I was so upset by everything and so distraught over the reaction of the family that I didn't tell anybody about these things I had found, and I thought the only one who would understand everything would be me, so I threw them all away, both rings and that piece of paper—that last note.

She had her reasons, of course. Not the least of these was that if she was carrying a child, she would have to face the family. She couldn't have lived through it because of the shame that those things brought on at that time. She knew that Dad would believe that she had ruined her life, just as his own sister had done. And I think she was conflicted over her relationship with Eddie. She liked him, but it's clear she wasn't in love, and I believe that she had misgivings about having a relationship with a Hispanic. From what I've told you about Frieda's response, you can guess that the family would have disapproved of her marrying someone from a different race. It was part of the culture back there, to marry your own kind.

Naturally, Irma took it incredibly hard. After all, she had become Emma's mother after the tragedy at the well. And I think she tried to convince everyone back there that it was an accident. As I said, Frieda finally believed me, I think. When I visited everyone back home, I talked to Carla about it. We lay on her bed and cried together. I think she was realistic. Gretchen says it will always remain a mystery—she was the diplomat, the peacemaker of the family. But Margaret and some of her children still believe that it was murder. As for Carl, I tried to talk to him soon after about the realities that I knew and felt, but when we got together about six months after this happened, he said, "Laura, I want you to know right from the start that I don't believe she committed suicide." And he wouldn't discuss it further.

⊱⊰

I had known about my Aunt Emma's suicide from the time I was a teen-ager. But until my mother's revelations, I had not appreciated the crushing impact of her sister's death. By understanding clearly the context in which Emma met her demise, I began to grasp the depth of psychological assault that my mother had endured as a wave of compressed events sent her on an emotional roller coaster. I was beginning to understand my mother and her rearing of me under the influence of the residue of her unspoken grief, her fear of loss, her guilt. Finally, finally, things were starting to make sense.

Here is the scenario as I see it:

Emma dons a mask of happiness before shocking everyone by taking her own life. She has learned to hide her feelings cleverly. As the youngest child, the family protects her, along with the other younger siblings, from the wretchedness of their mother's institutionalization in a mental hospital. She is the youngest child in a family of eight—smart, good-looking, self-confident. She sets high moral and academic standards for herself. To her family, she embodies all the hopes and dreams of the entire family. She is the mythic vessel into which is poured all hope for deliverance.

Embedded in her soul is the knowledge that she is the one chosen to erase all of the shame, to rise above all the misery of mental illness. No one tells her, "Emma, we have this really weird family, and you have to exonerate all of us from the shame and stigma of having a mentally ill mother," but she feels it as though it were spoken. But who can live up to the responsibility of liberating a family from its dark secrets? You hide the hurt and shame, and you are expected to help the family rise above it all. Ultimately, you feel as though you have failed, that it's your fault, that you've done something wrong.

Emma moves out to the Southwest, secures a teaching position and lives near my mother and father. She has two romances, but her heart remains with her college sweetheart with whom she secretly and daringly corresponds, although he is married.

My mother suffers the loss of a long-awaited baby seven months into the pregnancy and is denied any opportunity for open grieving. Emma has been at her side during this ordeal, along with my father. Together, they collude to shelter my mother from overwhelming sadness. In denying my mother the chance to mourn the loss of this baby girl openly, Emma acts out a family pattern of over protectiveness and control, which works to shield the protector from pain and guilt under the guise of helping the protected. With little time to grieve, my mother becomes pregnant with another baby—me—and begins to focus on her future as a contented mother. Her attention shifts to the child growing within her and away from Emma and all her personal problems. But the joy is short-lived. Four months after my birth, Emma changes everyone's lives by committing suicide. My mother suspects that possibly Emma was pregnant, but there is no proof, only cryptic clues.

Compounding my mother's devastation is the reaction of her family back home, who refuse to believe that Emma has died by her own hand. No way, was the first reaction, reflecting total denial. After all, the family has placed all of its hopes and expectations on Emma. To accept the truth that she took her own life is to admit that they have failed. And so, they deny the truth and convince themselves that some external cause is responsible.

By unfortunate timing, I am thrust into this drama, like it or not. I can no longer distance myself from this history. As chance would have it, I am entwined in it.

჻ৎ৯

By this time, Mother and I are taping the stories in New Mexico. Fourteen years have passed since we first began on that bright September day in San Diego. We have now finished another intense and revealing session. The shreds of old stories are starting to form themselves into one coherent whole. The interviews are set aside for now, and we are sitting on my mother's patio in the late afternoon, sipping tea, facing the mountains east of Albuquerque.

Starting about ten million years ago, massive fractures uplifted the earth's crust along a fault line, producing our magnificent view. For some time, great underground stirrings—the moving of geologic plates over time—weakened fragile cracks in the earth's strata. At several points over millions of years, the earth buckled, causing a massive heaving upwards, much like a trap door. But this was no violent, volcanic, spontaneous eruption. Rather, it was a gradual process defined by periodic pressures from several sources, characterized by heaving, collapsing and heaving again. At the foot of these great mountains, the earth gradually compacted to form a great basin, blanketed with layers of silt and rocks from which a fine city would grow. I could not help but think of my aunt's struggles, so buried, so cleverly covered. Yet all the while, underneath lay a psychic fragility ready to split apart, not unlike those weakened portions of the earth, where small but continuous ruptures coalesced only to be assailed at the breaking point by unstoppable forces. However, one human factor made things emphatically different from natural processes: intent.

Mother and I stretch out in our lounge chairs, hoping to see yet another gorgeous Southwest sunset. The temperature drops, the afternoon heat begins to dissipate, and now a cool breeze fans our faces. The sun dips behind the volcanoes to the west, and the Sandia Mountains begin to glow pink. Peach and coral splash over the western sky. Quickly, the pink on the mountains fades to slate blue as the sun retreats. No thunderstorms tonight— perhaps tomorrow. Dots of lights emerge here and there as the city prepares for evening rituals.

The mountains appear as a backdrop, a cardboard stage set behind a curtain hiding all the laborious work that has happened over time. And suddenly, we begin to murmur to each other about all we have shared, to talk in ways that we have not done in years. To break the tension, we joke about our foibles and resurrect old memories, reaching for tissues more than once. I tell her that I am beginning to understand the roots of the emotional distance between us, and that I wish to be forgiven for harboring grudges against her. She admits that she often expected too much from me too early—that she was a perfectionist. And I tell her that I hope she will forgive herself for not recognizing how deep Emma's troubles were, and for the wounding she believes that she inflicted upon my aunt.

As I let it all spill out, I long for the story to have a different outcome, an alternate script. I think of how lovely it would be if Emma could be right here with us, talking, laughing, drinking tea amidst the aching beauty of it all—the sky, the mountains, and the camaraderie of kindred spirits. I do not mention these inward feelings to my mother, but rather try to concentrate on savoring this one painful but beautiful moment. I am hoping that when the cloudscapes gather around the mountain's ridges and thunder rumbles during the monsoon season, the rains will wash away all the horror, all the harm and all the hurt.

But of course, there are only the two of us this evening, and here we are, talking softly, realizing that we are unwitting characters in dramas great and small, prodigious and personal. Before us, in the mountain's shadow, the city stretches out on waves of ancient sand reminding us of that desolate desert some fifty years before, where Emma's demons took hold, where she walked into the shooting range and pulled the trigger that ended her life. She was twenty-nine years old.

Part Two—Redemption

Once you have tasted flight, you will forever walk the earth with your eyes turned skyward, for there you have been, and there you will always long to return.

—Leonardo da Vinci

Poetry is a means of redemption.

—Wallace Stevens

Laura as student nurse circa 1926

Chapter 9

How an Angel Got Her Wings

… Our own little pixie
Never took a note in class, 'and still the wonder grew
that one small head could carry all she knew.'[1]
A penchant for the ministry, and picnics out of paper pokes behind
the yard palings. Adored for her cunning profile, gentle running
speech and her engaging whimsies … .

—Description of Laura Catherine Delaney
Yale School of Nursing Yearbook, 1928
(Each class member was characterized with a literary flair.)

None of them understood why I did it, why I left home and went to Yale. It spoke to my mind and my heart, as I told you. One of the things I was sure of—if I got out in the world, I could make my mistakes and do my trial swims among strangers. At home, I was so embarrassed when I made a mistake in front of people who knew me. But if I got out among people who didn't know me, I could speak my thoughts without fear of being made fun of.

Frieda never did totally understand what made me tick. But I know she loved me, and I can tell you something she shared with me. After a stroke she suffered in her late eighties, she told me, "I had a dream about you, Laura, that you were going to a far country and you took me with you." I think that all this time, a part of her wanted to get out, but of course, she stayed. She married and had a comfortable life financially, far better than mine, but you know all about that. Although she didn't grasp my yearnings, Frieda was a fountain of good will. I leaned on her,

---

1   Parody on line from the poem "The Deserted Village," by Oliver Goldsmith (1730-1774) — " … and still the wonder grew, that one small head could carry all he knew."

probably too much. That's another reason why I realized I should try my wings.

I had already begun to learn when I first started high school that there was something out there—knowledge—that I deeply wanted. I was thirsty for it. The day I left for Yale, Gretchen drove me to Clarkton to catch a train. By that time, she was teaching, so she had a vehicle. I had already learned enough about the train when I took those summer courses. And I had read up on train travel. The route took us to New York City overnight, and I arranged for a sleeper car. I was confident, and the porters were wonderful, so helpful and considerate. When I got to New York City, there was supposed to be a friend, someone we had known in Norton who had moved to New York, who would meet me at the information desk at Grand Central Station. I waited and waited, but she was a no show, so there I was, stuck by myself in the busiest train station in the country. I wasn't too scared though, because the red caps came tumbling toward me to take the luggage. I told one of them what train I was taking to New Haven and said, "Thank you." I was thinking what wonderful service the train companies offered. But he stood around awkwardly and finally said, "Lady, we usually get something for our services." I asked how much, if you can imagine! I blush to think about it now, how ignorant I was. Well, I finally realized that he was angling for a tip, and, oh, I don't know, I think I gave him a dollar. That was quite a bit in those days. I know I made a lot of silly hillbilly mistakes. Not surprisingly, from that point on, the red caps became my friends. I boarded the train to New Haven and took a taxi to the campus.

I remember two things about that first night. First, how happy I was to be able to take a shower! It was my first. We did have a bathtub in Norton, but, oh, what luxury, to have that water pouring all over me. I'm getting a little ahead of myself, but the girls told me of the benefits of taking cold showers, if you can believe it. I modified that suggestion by taking a hot shower every morning and finishing it off with a cold dash of water. The amazing thing about that is you don't feel the outside cold as much. On those chilly days, I would walk with one of the teachers in the morning to the first place of instruction. Even when the snow was flying, we would be seen in just our uniforms and our nurses' hats clipped to the side of our foreheads, with no coats or scarves because we had taken those cold showers.

The other thing that happened—remember, I told you about the ruby engagement ring that Irma sold to me? I was so proud of that ring! Well, on my first night in the dorm, I stupidly left it on my dresser, and I suppose that the maid stole it while I was down at dinner. When I told the housemother the next day, she was snippy and informed me that she couldn't watch everybody and that I would have to protect my own valuables. I learned quickly that I was too trusting. I had lost the ring, but I was the cause of it. For a while I was awfully embarrassed—and depressed.

I knew I had to toughen up. So from the day I arrived, I began to show some independence. For starters, I went downtown and got my hair cut. Back home, it was thought that you were a floozy if you bobbed your hair. I suppose my sisters and Dad would have been horrified. But I did it anyway. To get some style, we used a waver instrument. You could heat it and it would produce pretty waves in your hair. You can see how I look, short hairstyle and stylish clothes in that picture I had taken upon graduating –the one in which I'm wearing the fur cape.

There were eleven of us girls in that hall. We were all in the same class. Each of us had our own room, and we had alternative hours being on and off duty. We ate together in the common dining hall. There was a housemother, an old-fashioned New England spinster, and she made a house into a home. The living room was quite nice with a wood-burning fireplace, and every afternoon she served tea—we could take one lump or two of sugar. We could sit down and talk to anyone else there. As you can guess, I was about as far as one could get from the living conditions on the farm and later the house in Norton. I was only one of two without a bachelor's degree. Some of the girls came from prestigious colleges—Wellesley, Radcliffe, Mt. Holyoke among others. As it turned out, I held my own, at least academically. But I did struggle with all those, you know, social cues, but I was not excluded. We all accepted each other—there were no cliques. We were there to learn.

We were only the third class. Dean Annie Goodrich was a founder of the idea of educated nursing, that a nurse should be educated rather than trained. She was revered within the whole profession. Not only was she the first woman dean of YSN but also later became the first woman dean of Yale University. I was indeed fortunate. She is the one who had written right back to me and accepted me as a scholarship student. I don't think that kind of financial support is available these days. How I cherished the memory of those "Class Dinners with the Dean" at her home and our prim "bread and butter calls"[2] the next day! Always in our white gloves, of course. We all adored her.

Before I tell you about the other girls and how we became friends, I guess I have to say that during that first year, I often felt so alone, that I was fending for myself. I had to battle the old fears and self-doubts, and I worried excessively about myself and my personality. Although my fellow classmates liked me—I'm sure of it—I continued to feel different—that sense of inferiority hadn't changed. I may have thought I could pitch away those feelings in a new setting, but it didn't work quite that way. As we got into psychiatric training, I began to question whether I had some sort of psychopathic personality. That might have been natural, given how much I was like Mother.

The second year was better. But at first, I had a mental hygiene battle, so I practiced something I had come across in a book—"Every day in every way, I am getting better and better." I read about how you could get a rope, tie knots in it and say this every time you touched a knot, going around the whole circle, like a rosary. Now I know what a rosary does for people.

The relationships—you must know, it was not like a college sorority. It was a work situation. We would visit occasionally in the evening, mostly coming from class. We were closer because we worked together. Oh, we talked with each other occasionally, but we were busy and often on duty, so it wasn't like we were in each other's rooms gabbing all the time. Still, we became quite fond of one another. They would gently tease me about my rural

---

2   "Bread and butter" letters are thank-you notes sent by guests to a host or hostess who has invited them to her or his home. In this case, the student nurses were expected to deliver their appreciation in person to the Dean on the day following the event.

expressions, like "palings" for "picket fences" and "pokes" for paper bags. I learned not to blush but to take their ribbing as a sign they really cared for me.

I did make two important friendships that lasted me beyond those years. Kathryn took me under her wing from the start. All the girls were fixing up their rooms, but I had no extra money to do that. She suggested that we go downtown and select material—she paid for it—and we sewed up some nice curtains and a matching bedspread. To make me feel that I was not a charity case, Kathryn told me that she would learn better if someone would read the text to her, so she had me do that and paid me for it. She tried to cast it that you were helping her out, not the other way around.

Kathryn came from a well-to-do family in Minnesota, but she was mostly wealthy in heart. She remained a friend until the end of her life. She had told me that her estate from her father was larger than she had expected and to please rely on her if necessary. I took care not to abuse that trust, but there were a couple of times when I did call on this generous offer. After I went out to Arizona, I was offered a position as a combination school nurse and teacher. There wasn't the public transportation that I became used to in New Haven, and there was no way to get to school. So I needed a car. I swallowed my pride and borrowed the money from her and faithfully paid her back with good interest.

One time she visited me in New Mexico around 1950, and she noticed that I had a goiter—that's a tumor on the thyroid gland—growing large around my neck. I didn't broach the issue with her, but it was obvious that I would need surgery. But we had no money, and insurance was unheard of. She told me straight, without my ever mentioning it, to let her know if I needed to have an operation. So when the doctor said that I really did need to attend to this, I wrote her, and she sent the money. Again, I took it as a loan and slowly paid her back. As you recall, those were tough times for us. There were times that I could only manage sending the interest, which I did faithfully. And over time, I got the entire loan retired. You know, things are so different these days. With Kathryn, I believe it was in her makeup to want to share. It seemed to make her feel genuinely good about herself when she was helping out. But she made it out that you were doing her the favor. As I said, she was a classy lady.

Somehow, she picked me out from the beginning as a person in need of a guide, a friend, a mentor. Kathryn would say, "Be my guest at a play or concert. I can't go alone and would love the company." So, often we would take the train down from New Haven to New York City. That's how I saw Fritz Kreisler the violinist playing his own works *Liebesleid* and *Liebesfreud* and heard Galli-Curci, the famous Italian coloratura soprano.

I saw Will Rogers on stage twirling his rope and attended lots of plays. Seeing Helen Hayes in "What Every Woman Knows" remains in my memory as a favorite experience.

I was hungry for culture, and I tried to visit every gallery, every museum available. You could go all over New Haven in those days by streetcar. If one of the other girls couldn't go with me, I'd go by myself. You could do that without fear of being mugged. And I soaked it all up. We'd had Lyceum courses in high school and the Chautauqua lectures on the hospital grounds, but this was the real thing. I felt I was walking on clouds when we visited the famous museums in New York City. I remember the first time I saw this Renoir painting in the Museum of Modern Art. It was of a woman sitting by the seashore in a hat and blue dress. I had longed to see the ocean, and this painting made me want to do that even more. When I had first arrived in New Haven, I told the girls about my wish. So they made sure that I got my longed for view of the Atlantic. It took my breath away, just like that painting.

The other friend I kept up with after graduation was Marjorie. I hated her at first. At one point, we got moved from one dorm room to another, and I had lined up my shoes under the bed. I don't know where else we could have put them. Anyhow, when the bed got pushed aside, she saw them and laughed. Oh, was I red-faced. She had made fun of me, with echoes of my father. I couldn't stand her. But, you know, she turned out to be a good friend.

Now I had always been attracted to people who could use words well and express themselves with great articulation. That was because I so often found myself tongue-tied and didn't want to speak up. Marjorie had a master's degree and had taught languages in high school before coming to Yale. My goodness, could she sling the King's English! Her mother had been a New York City school teacher, prim and proper with much religiosity. Marjorie had to struggle with some of the same issues that I had. She later told me that she didn't know whether she believed in "Sin," with a capital letter. I guess I knew what she meant. Anyhow, one summer evening, we went for a walk and lay down in the grass somewhere on the campus. And for the first time, I began to express what was inside of me. It all tumbled out, the residue of all the religious stuff—the trauma—because I had never told anyone. It was such a relief to let some of this out. I had thrown it all over when I was about seventeen, but there were still these terrible fears lingering deep in my soul—would I commit a sin before I was forgiven? Was I saved? All that other stuff I told you about. She listened and seemed to understand. Later, Marjorie told everyone, "Laura and I have revived the art of conversation." She and I became close from that point on.

If you met Marjorie, you'd probably think she was a "weirdo," but she had great perceptiveness and an astute brain. But she certainly had her troubles. It turned out that she was manic-depressive—I think they call it bipolar these days. I would hear her say, "I'm low in my mind. I wish I was dead." I felt sorry for her; she knew she was different in this way. The psychiatric training that we had was among the first in any of the nursing schools. It was through this exposure that Marjorie figured out that she had some deep problems. This was recognized and she entered treatment. I don't think there were any medications, only for psychotic patients, so I'm not sure what the treatment consisted of—probably psychological counseling.

You asked about our courses, the curriculum and the experiences. We had orthopedics, the isolation ward, emergency room, obstetrics, surgery, ear-nose-throat, pediatrics and psychiatry. We also paired up with the Visiting Nurses Association. We went out on home visits, and let me tell you, some of those homes were upsetting, quite dirty. We would have to give baths, change sheets and instruct the families on how to care for their sick children.

Besides classes, we spent much time on duty in the university's hospital, which was part of the medical school. We all started with what was called the "Pre-clinic term." That's where we learned how to give bed baths, change beds, and how to be a bedside nurse. Next, we went on the wards. On my first day, I was sent to a man's ward. First patient I had, I had to insert a rectal tube. Oh, I thought I would die! I asked the head nurse as humbly as I could if I could be re-assigned to a woman's ward. She consulted the supervisor, but they decided—in their infinite wisdom, no doubt—that it was better for me to continue where I was. Talk about baptism by fire! Another one—once during an ER rotation, a man from the Italian quarter was brought in all slashed up, covered with blood. This was in 1926 and Mussolini had been made prime minister of Italy and taken the title of Il Duce. Anyhow, this man was a bit crazy, and he was shouting and babbling about shooting Mussolini! That was my baptism by blood.

Once when I was in charge of the obstetrics ward, I was coming up the stairs one night and I heard someone call, "Noirsh! Noirsh!" I knew what had happened. This woman, who had had about twelve babies already, was in the bathroom. And there was the baby—it had been born in a bedpan. We nurses were not supposed to cut the cord ourselves, so all the nurses under me scurried around and got everything ready for the doctors to do that. I noticed that baby's head was up, and I asked her why because they're usually born face turned down. She told me she had reached down and turned it over. And that was that.

We weren't allowed to deliver babies, nor was it part of our formal education. That was only for the doctors. We were only taught how to clean up the mother. There was one baby that was stillborn, and I had to take care of it—that was a bad experience. I remember my amazement the first time I saw a baby born. Of course I knew where they came from, but you don't account for how you'll feel when you witness your first birth. For someone who was told until she was twelve years old that babies were dropped into the house by the doctor, this was all plenty amazing to me.

In pediatrics, I witnessed a Jewish circumcision. Before that, I had watched a regular circumcision being performed. You had to check the little boy babies every morning and retract the foreskin. If it was too tight and wouldn't retract, the doctors gave them a circumcision. Oh, that poor little baby lay there and bled, and it must have been really painful. So they sent us student nurses down to witness this Jewish circumcision. The rabbi had these special instruments—they would get them all ready and position this instrument around the penis and do the prick really fast. There was little blood and no pain. At least it seemed that way. But I guess these rabbis are experts at it. They've done it for thousands of years. Now there are books and articles about how there's no reason to circumcise, that it's barbaric, part of cultural history. I don't know how I feel about that, but one thing's for sure—if I were a man, I'd take the Jewish kind.

We also had instruction in psychiatry. Now you may be wondering if I felt peculiar during psychiatric training because of Mother. Basically, I tried to consider myself a normal person, but I knew in my heart of hearts that I was awfully strange. I tried to remove my emotions from it and focus on becoming a good nurse. I could see on the "better wards" like my mother's situation, that there were different grades and stages of illnesses. And I saw that Mother was in much better shape than some of the patients I saw. As I told you, she was logical, not out of her mind. I suppose I should have been torn up by this part of our training, but I took it in stride. When I look back, I realize that I bottled up a huge amount of feeling and tried desperately to cut off my emotions and memories. I know I must have blocked out the trauma. I had to, to survive in the program and move forward.

The professor of psychiatry once brought to our lecture class a man from the mental ward and proceeded to ask him questions. After the man left, he asked the class of nurses what they noticed. I was kind of raw in this sort of stuff, but the girls who were more sophisticated spoke up and said that this patient had all eyes on the doctor. The professor described it as homosexual feelings. During this time, they thought such people were psychotic, and that's why this man had been placed in a mental institution. I shudder to think about the fine people who were mistaken for being mentally ill when they were simply following their own nature. But I didn't reason it out deeply enough. And if any of us had thought differently, not one of us would ever have considered questioning our professors' authority. That would be *verboten*.

And that brings me to another reminiscence. It was at Yale that I got my first introduction to lesbianism. Two of our women professors—one was a horsey lady who practically galloped into the classroom, and the other one was quite girlish—it was rumored about that they were, uh ... attached. Those were the whisperings, and I didn't pay too much attention—I didn't really know much about those sorts of things.

But I'm sure about two in our class, that they were women lovers. One of them, Millicent was her name, was a sophisticated girl from Boston, a graduate from one of the top women's colleges there. She had done volunteer medical social work. Her family was quite wealthy but also restrictive, and she came to Yale, I believe, to get away from them when they urged her to marry. The other girl, Evelyn, was the adopted daughter of a college professor. But poor Evelyn, she was so naïve. Her parents had kept her innocent. From the start, Millicent practically nabbed Evelyn, and they became constant companions. We knew that they spent time in each other's rooms during off-duty time. Some of us other girls were quite uneasy because Millicent really mistreated and imposed upon Evelyn. For instance, they would make plans to go out, and Millicent would snub her and not show up for the "date." She would go gallivanting to parties and whatnot but would never apologize for standing up a friend! Things like that.

After they graduated, Millicent's family took her on a trip to Europe. No doubt they felt they could still win her back. And if you can believe this, in the middle of the Atlantic Ocean,

Millicent got stubborn and insisted she was going back home, so the family arranged for her to get on another ship and return to the United States! I guess they realized that their efforts were going to be futile, so they gave into her wishes. She got back together with Evelyn, and they both got jobs together in a hospital. They got an apartment together, and they worked in the same places. When Millicent died, Evelyn lived only six months after that. I got all this information in dribs and drabs over the years. I don't know if they sexualized their relationship, but it was clear that they were a couple. Marjorie was the one who educated me. She had street smarts and taught me a lot.

As I said, we attended classes in addition to the job training. The professors were quite exacting in all ways. Once in eye-ear-nose and throat class, we had an exam on eye irritation— blepharitis. This happened at a time when I was dealing with a failed romance and wasn't paying too much attention to the lecture. So, on the exam I spelled it with an "f" instead of a "ph" and the professor was so disgusted with me and showed that paper to the head nurse. I had been a schoolteacher and knew it should have been a "ph," so I was disgusted with myself. And wouldn't you know, I now suffer from blepharitis! I suppose you could say it's poetic justice.

Remember that complimentary blurb under my picture in the yearbook—the one that read "Never took a note in class ... "? Well, the story started a bit unpleasantly with one of the nurse lecturers. The doctors didn't know—or care—if we took notes. But the nurse lecturers were maiden ladies and proud of their ability to lecture, and you should be able to take notes. It had been my habit ever since high school and on through my two-year teaching degree to take notes as an outline. Anyhow, she noticed I wasn't writing every word and she called me on it. "Don't you take notes on my lecture, Miss Delaney?" I responded in truth, "Yes, in outline form." She didn't call on me again, but the others were impressed.

While on duty in the isolation ward, I got chicken pox. The supervisor on this ward blamed me. In isolation, you're not supposed to catch anything—you had to scrub, you couldn't

touch a patient. You used a paper towel—paper towels were our
friends—to pick up the cups or anything that was served in the
meals. The super herself had said that measles and chicken pox
could be caught through the air. I woke up one morning covered
with blisters. "You broke training," she said. I recall that she
scolded me royally. So they made me stay in isolation until the
last pimple was gone. The fear was that it could be smallpox, and
I hadn't been vaccinated. So they vaccinated me, and I still have
that scar on my leg.

We student nurses worked hard, but there were lots of
extracurricular activities, too. There were various parties held at
the dorms for the medical students. Knowing my personality, you
can understand that I didn't enjoy those too much. But one thing
I do recall fondly. There was a cottage at the seashore, which
was maintained by the University. The school really tried to
make us happy and comfortable. Two of the girls had cars—one
was Kathryn. She called her Dodge automobile "Fat Chance."
We had a great time driving down to the cottage with her. We
took food with us or ate out. Oh, and I must mention also the
football games at the Yale Bowl, which was close to our dorm.
I often went by myself when no one else was interested. One
time I walked over to the stadium and watched the Army-Navy
game. Army paraded around their mascot, a white mule, and it
stalled right in front of the Navy section and, well, let loose! I'll
bet they stimulated it to do it. I'm telling you, the whole crowd
roared with laughter!

As I neared graduation, I knew for sure—these had been the
happiest days of my life.

Laura after graduation late 1928

Chapter 10

Memorabilia

From The Yale School of Nursing (YSN) Yearbook, 1928

*After we talked about the Yale years, my mother showed me her
yearbook from the graduating class of 1928. Tucked amongst the
pages were two 3 X 5 cards in her handwriting and one yellowed
letter. One card noted that she had contributed an original essay,
"How the Angels Got Their Wings"³ in which the main character, a
student nurse, pokes gentle fun at everything from pompous lectures
to professors to board members. The other card mentioned that she
collaborated with another student in writing the spoof, "How to Move
a Patient from One Mattress to Another." Both pieces appear in this
chapter.*

*The letter was from the Dean of Yale University, James Angell,
who complimented the Dean of the Nursing School on a charming
production (the yearbook).*

*These nurses were good writers, familiar with English poets,
novelists and essayists. And there is a touch of early feminist rebellion
slyly embedded in their ventures into literary productions.*

*What surprises me most is the emergence of some unlikely traits,
which I realize had been suppressed for years: a sense of humor and
wicked wit. By having her work published and her contributions
valued, my mother was beginning to be appreciated for her gifts and
talents.*

---

3   This essay is a mixed parody of tales from Rudyard Kipling's *Just So Stories*,
originally published in 1902, (Cf. "The Sing Song of Old Man Kangaroo" – "he went
to Nqa at six before breakfast, saying, 'Make me different from all other animals by
five this afternoon.'") and Lewis Carroll's *Alice in Wonderland*, published in 1865
(Cf. Chapter 2, which opens, "'Curiouser and curiouser!' cried Alice.'" and Chapter
3, where a major character is a Mouse. The White Mouse may be a blend of this
character and also the White Rabbit).

Nancy Key Roeder

HOW THE ANGELS GOT THEIR WINGS

PART ONE

In the high and far-off times, O, Best Beloved, the nurse was not as you see her now. She was not educated. She was sweet, and she was girlish, and her pride was inordinate, and she went to the Academy and said: "Make me different from all other creatures. Make me an educated nurse."

The Academy held up its hands in horror and shouted: "Go away! We can teach you all about evolution and the modern poetry, but we cannot make you an educated nurse."

She was young, and she was trusting, and her pride was inordinate, and she went to the School of Experience and said: "Make me different from all other creatures. Make me also wonderfully useful. Make me an educated nurse."

But the School of Experience rose up from its place among the ash cans and said: "Don't bother me! I can teach her how to wash pans and scrape kettles, but I can't be bothered with all this tom-foolery!"

She was piqued but yet persistent. She put on her sailor hat and her least business manner, and she went to the great god Rockefeller[4], and she said: "Make me different from all other creatures. Make me very useful as well as very knowing. Make me an educated nurse."

She almost wept with joy when he shook her hand vigorously and shouted: "I will."

So he bade her say goodbye to her very doubting family, and he set her down quite roughly in the middle of New Haven. He was gone and there was about her only strangeness and a great loneliness. Suddenly there appeared before her this mystic symbol: "Y.S.N." Her heart sang with recognition and she ran toward it.

And that, O, Beloved of Mine, is the first part of the tale.

---

4   The Yale School of Nursing was originally funded by the Rockefeller Foundation. It was the first autonomous school of nursing with its own dean, faculty, budget, and degree that had to meet the standards of the University. The mission departed from then existing nursing programs by stressing an education path rather than on the service needs of hospitals.

PART TWO

When the nurse came to herself she realized that a great door had opened and was just closing behind her. Her first impulse was to flee, but finding that impossible she looked about her and her eye fell upon the directory of the building. Here it is as she remembered it:

Medicine

Surgery

Phrenology

Osteopathy

Pediatrics

Just as she was thinking how long it would take her to go through all these rooms, the large directory board swung outward on a hinge and before she knew it, it had clicked behind her.

"Curiouser and curiouser," thought the nurse, for as her eye became accustomed to the semi-darkness she realized that what she had thought was an ordinary building was really a maze. She had always had a horror of being lost in a maze, and she was just sitting down to shed a gallon of tears when she saw ahead of her a queer little creature on a gold-plated pedestal. She hurried after it and when she came nearer to it she saw that it was a little white mouse with a tiny white cap set proudly between its ears. Just as she was about to speak to it, it darted through the door. As she quickly opened the door to follow, she saw written over it, "Pre-Clinic Term." [5]

When the door had closed behind them, the little creature turned, peered benignly down upon her and said, "Guess what is in my mind."

The nurse was not accustomed to reading people's minds, and she said so, whereupon the little creature replied that she would have to get used to "thinking things through" if she were ever to get out of this maze.

---

5   This 28-month nursing program was divided into three terms: Pre-Clinic, Juniors and Seniors.

Then it handed her a little card upon which was a diagram, which she guessed to be the plot of the maze.

"Now," it said, "there are a great many ways out of here, and you must think, and decide which way you will choose."

So the nurse thought and thought. By and by, when she had it all thought out, the little mouse said: "Now you can choose any of these ways which you want so long as you choose my way."

There was nothing left to do but to agree, and the nurse took up her journey after White Mouse. And there ends the second part of the tale.

PART THREE

Still went White Mouse scampering on ahead of her, never looking backward, darting through the winding ways. Still ran Yale Nurse, running after White Mouse, never getting nearer, never getting farther, peering through the darkness, groping through the hallways.

And as she ran these are some of the remarks she made:—(she must not be impolite to White Mouse)—"Isn't this a heavenly maze!" "That little cap you have on is as cute as a bug's ear. I care for that." "Do we really do bedside nursing?" "What does appendectomy mean?" "Do we really have an eight hour day?" "We shall all be hospital superintendents when we get through here."

To all of these questions and observations the smiling creature elucidatingly made answer:

"The relation of the nurse to the community health program from a public health point of view requires the adjustment to the environment of the family as a unit of society and a knowledge of poverty as a social and economic aspect of disease only recovered from by the proper application of the principles of case work to experience records."

For that, O, Beloved of Mine, is the way all little white mice on gold-plated pedestals always talk.

Soon stopped White Mouse by a high doorway. Over this doorway were the letters, "Juniors."

Still came Yale Nurse, close upon White Mouse, never catching up to her, always just around the corner, puzzleder and puzzleder, always searching blindly, ever groping madly to find her way out of the maze. She had to.

And now as she came, she was heard to make some such observations as these:

"Life is hard and there is no justice." "O, my ego and my smashed metatarsal arches!" "Just to get my feet up." "Am I really setting precedents?" "O, these inputs and out-takes." "I was certain it looked like cresol[6] in that sponge-stick jar."

And the White Mouse went on ahead muttering: "My watch and scissors, but you are slow! You don't take your responsibilities seriously enough, and you are not seeing the maze as a whole!"

On ran White Mouse, cunning little White Mouse, on its gold-plated pedestal, puffing like a white mouse would puff. It had to.

Then came Yale Nurse, first walking carefully with the blue guidebook, following quite soberly—and she fell farther and farther behind. Then flinging the blue guidebook over her shoulder and donning her roller skates, she began to cut corners. She had to.

And thus they arrived at a large arched gateway marked "Seniors."

The gate swung slowly and solemnly back. The nurse walked in, close by the side of White Mouse. Inside there was an innumerable company of animals and birds of all kinds who looked friendly and were good enough to say to nurse that they were very glad to see her, and that they hoped that she would be a guide to all those who came after her, to help them get through the maze without too much resistance. Senior Nurse wanted to say that she did not know the way out, and that she could hardly, therefore, guide anybody else. But she thought that might sound disrespectful so she said nothing. Looking ahead, she saw that White Mouse had taken advantage of the pause and was many paces ahead.

---

6   Cresol is a chemical with several applications in medicine. It has a reddish-brown tint. Although used in the past as a disinfectant in surgery, it has largely been displaced by less toxic substances.

Away went Senior Nurse following after White Mouse, and as she started, the impetus of her flight knocked over two or three of the birds and animals that were the weakest. But she said: "Excuse my dust," (by this time, O Best Beloved, she was growing slightly impertinent) and went flying after White Mouse. She had to.

Now she came nearer, now she fell farther behind, and as she fitfully came nearer and fell farther behind, these are some of the fragments of their conversation, and sometimes it was talked and sometimes it was shouted:

White Mouse: "You're very neurotic."

Yale Nurse: "That is just my ego."

White Mouse: "You're too officious, as well as quite conceited."

Yale Nurse: "I hate to think it's all in my glands."

White Mouse: "You should study the relation of the nurse to the community filth campaign."

Yale Nurse: "Well, laugh that off!"

White Mouse: "What patient are you going to take for your case study?"

Yale Nurse: "I have an idea, but I'm sure it's crazy."

White Mouse: "I must tell you that one of the Lady Board Members doesn't like your uniform."

Yale Nurse: "My deah! I was so chagrined!"

White Mouse: "I should like to have a conference with you. You have been disrespectful to your superiors, et cetera, et cetera."

Yale Nurse: "F'eaven's sake!"

"And now," said White Mouse, as they arrived at an expansive portal marked 'Community,' "we have come to the end of the maze."

And they both sat down very hard and said, "Thank goodness that is finished."

And the mouse said: "Before I open this door which will mean your final release from the maze, I want to tell you that there is a great future in store for you."

"That's because I'm a very remarkable fellow," said Yale Nurse.

And the only sound that came back to White Mouse is it passed out beyond the pale, and started scampering back to guide other wondering travelers through, was the echo:

" 'Markable fellow!' "

HOW TO MOVE A PATIENT FROM ONE MATTRESS TO ANOTHER

PRE-CLINICAL TERM

Object: To accomplish a "good piece of work" with the least exertion, mental and physical for the head nurse.

Anatomical factors to be considered:

1. The length of the patient in relation to the length of the mattress.

2. The sensitivity of the patient to his own mattress dust.

Equipment:

Two bath blankets

Bath rubber

Percussion hammer

Tongue stick and paper bag

Hypodermic needle, syringe, and novocaine

One package large sponges

Scrub-up tray

Ice cap and hot water bottle

Procedures:

1. Nurse A places bath rubber under patient's arm and anaesthetizes her, while Nurse B takes a complete family history from the public health point of view.

2. Nurse B takes a complete family history from the public health point of view.

3. Nurses C and D bring new mattress from store room and place on bed beside patient.

4. Nurse B then examines patient's throat for enlarged tonsils, placing tongue stick in the paper bag afterward.

5. Nurse C wraps ice cap in bath blanket and puts to patient's feet.

6. Nurse D wraps hot water bottle in bath blanket and puts to patient's head.

7. Nurses A, B, C, and D then arrange themselves around patient and sing the Doxology.

8. Person in the next bed is requested to give patient three gentle raps on head with percussion hammer, while Nurses A, B, C, and D take three deep breaths and exhale deeply and slowly.

9. Nurse A counts "One, two, three." On "three" they all raise patient slowly in air until she is above other mattress. The fingers are then removed. If the procedure has been thought through correctly the patient will land in the middle of the mattress. (It has also been found to facilitate matters if the patient keeps her fingers crossed during the entire procedure.) The student nurse, however, should not be discouraged if, for the first few times when she performs the procedure, the patient at this point lands in the last bed on the opposite side of the ward or in the treatment room. Only practice assures accurate aim.

10. Take the patient's temperature, a blood count, and a Wasserman[7] and leave her with the latest copy of the *New Yorker*, and thankfulness in her heart.

HOW TO MOVE A PATIENT FROM ONE MATTRESS TO ANOTHER
JUNIOR YEAR

Patient walks to empty bed.
Nurse writes note to (nursing supervisor).

---

7   Wasserman – antibody test for syphilis.

Chapter 11

Loves, Losses, Luck

Too many tears for lovers have been shed,
Too many sighs give we to them in fee,
Too much of pit after they are dead,
Too many doleful stories do we see,
Whose matter in bright gold were best be read.
> —John Keats, from *Isabella or The Pot of Basil*, verse XII

I was curious about my mother's love life before she met my father. She had revealed little—only a few recollections when talking about earlier "crushes." So I asked her whether she had any serious prospects during or after the Yale years, before meeting my father in Arizona. It turns out that by chance, I am here because the old stigma surrounding the family turned away a possible union.

So you want to know about my romantic life. I can tell you it was practically non-existent—it would be considered downright dull to modern women. But remember, I thought of myself as strange. My mind drove me to do all these things, like going off to Yale and soaking up culture. But I had this domestic side, too—you remember that I was the one to do the picnics for Mother. I guess the others cared, but they let me do it, and I didn't mind. And I told you how it was when my sisters went off to summer courses while I stayed home to take care of Margaret and Emma. It hurt me that they assumed I wouldn't want to go with them. But I was torn, too. I wanted so much to make a home for the little girls. I was a homebody but had this intensely inquisitive mind. I think I was two people in one body. A professor of mine—he was head of extension courses for teachers headquartered in Norton—told me, "You are one-half masculine and one-half feminine. You have a man's mind. If you do have a date, inevitably your mind will show up over your femininity and it will be off." That's the way men looked at things, you know. But a lot of what he said was true.

While we were still on the farm, there was a "beau" from our local church. I met him at one of the revival meetings, just before Mother had her tragedy. But, oh, I was such a prude! He wanted to go on to something serious. We had a few dates, walks. He would come the next summer to Norton and pay visits. When he left, he asked if I would kiss him goodbye. I told him I didn't believe in kissing until you became engaged. I had absorbed all those strict messages from the aunts and was shocked when he wanted a kiss from me. Can you imagine? He wrote me a couple of letters that I set aside and didn't answer.

There was also an engagement to a third cousin, Donald Longman. Did you hear about that one? This was right after high school, when I started teaching the next fall and boarded at Uncle Billy's place. Anyhow, Donald was distantly related to us—oh, I don't know exactly, a third cousin or something like that—but he was around all the time. He gave me my first kiss. We decided we would be married during the next summer. But, wouldn't you know, he came around to visit us in Norton right after school was out, and Margaret up and flirted with him and made eyes at him until he melted. Once that happened, he said nothing more to me about getting married. So that didn't work out, but lucky me! Margaret didn't marry him either. Honestly, he was rough and crude, and we were both better off without him.

It was in my second year of teaching that I had my first real heart-throb romance. I'm ashamed to tell you this now—but it was with one of my tenth grade students. He was sixteen. How foolish I was! Nothing really happened, and no one saw us together because we didn't let that be known. It was just my feelings of attraction toward him.

But I knew I should get away, so I found another job way out there in the sticks in a little town called Clapton. It was noted for a wildcat well that gushed oil into the sky. People couldn't

strike matches because oil ran down the creek banks. I had
to ride a horse part of the way to get to school—there was no
pavement. But you reached a point on top of a hill, where you
could see down the valley and know that the horse couldn't get
across all that thickness and come up the other side. You needed
a grapevine to swing in. Grapevines grew wild, and they were
often cut off for swings and jump ropes. You may not believe this,
but I actually did swing over the valley and onto the other side of
the hill—but not many times before I figured out that I couldn't
do that for the whole school year! Once you were on the other
side, you'd need a taxi to take you the rest of the way. The roads
were bumpy when dry, but when they were wet, the wheels could
sink in the clay. I didn't want to risk that every day, so I looked
for a family to room and board with, and I found one on the side
of the hill where the school was.

This family had a son, and he was the one who drove me
in for work. We were first associated as friends, but he took an
interest in me romantically. But oh, was I naïve! He wanted to
kiss me and staying firm in my beliefs, I told him I didn't believe
in that until two people were engaged. He talked to me about
getting married and about my getting a "womb protector." Oh
my, I was so uneducated in those things. And I told him. "Oh,
no, that would not be right, that you should only "do it" when
you wanted to have children. I have to laugh now, but what he
said was, "Well, that would really be hard on a man." As you can
imagine, this romance ended quickly!

And that's about the extent of any contact with the opposite
sex up until nurses' training. I began to think that I'd better
start having some kind of social life. By that time I was around
twenty-seven. I know I was afraid of becoming the dreaded "old
maid." I was skittish about it at first, but I started attending the
Methodist Church and joined the Young People's Association.
They didn't pretend to do anything except have discussions—no
guilt trips, nothing like that. They didn't think much about God.
They were too concerned about matters of associations between
boys and girls, how the girl sets the pace and so forth. You were
supposed to visit inside the home, not date outside of the home.
It was up to the girl to set the limits, that sort of thing. They

seemed more interested in those things and how to run their churches rather than in anything spiritual. But when they did mention God, it was a good, loving God. So there wasn't any reason to go back to those old fears. These ideas were coming out of the Divinity School.

I met Laurence at these meetings. He was taking medical training to become a physical therapist. We were in a play together, "Wedding Present," and he played the part of my fiancé. I know I was a foolish girl, but I fell head over heels for him. Kathryn brought roses to me after the play and winked. She had high hopes for me. Laurence and I had a few dates, and I really let my dreams get away with me. But it was clear—I can see that now—that I was not up to his station, his level of sophistication. He did not pursue the relationship. Not surprisingly, I was crushed. I had a rock in my chest day and night when I thought about it. Kathryn had started going with me to the YPA (Young People's Association), and she had better luck than I did because she met the man she later married.

Despite the heartache over Laurence, I continued going to the meetings. In my second year, I met Dan, and we started to date. He was in the School of Theology and planned to become a minister. He asked me about my philosophy of life, was I "the captain of my soul," as in the poem "Invictus" by Leonard Ernest Henley.[8] He wanted to know my philosophy—did God control my destiny or was I in control. I guess he was troubled that this poet seemed to be an agnostic or—heaven forbid—an atheist. He wanted to be sure which side I was on. But at that point, I wasn't thinking about a philosophy of life. I was *doing* life and, yes, trying to catch a man!

I didn't really fall for Dan, but we were nearing the end of our schooling and I definitely wanted to get married. I was frustrated that he hadn't proposed, but I felt that he *would* ask if I could be patient, and I was confident enough that I told the girls at Yale that we were about to become engaged. Remember the line in

---

8   Henley wrote the poem in 1875 (published in 1888) after having his leg amputated for tuberculosis of the bone. He held the stoic perspective that man, not a God, is in charge of his own fate. Famous last lines from this poem: "It matters not how strait the gate, how charged the punishments the scroll, I am the master of my fate: I am the captain of my soul."

the description of me in the yearbook, the one that reads, "A penchant for the ministry ... "? It refers to Dan and the belief among the girls that he and I would be getting engaged.

But graduation was nearing, and Dan still had not popped the question. I was at sea about it—having doubts about him as a future mate, but also feeling that same growing sense of rejection from yet another man. Things were not exactly off at that point, but drifting. I knew I had to get some sort of work, and it occurred to me that I might get on as a private duty nurse at Johns Hopkins Hospital in Baltimore. My sister Margaret lived out from Baltimore on a farm. She had married a farmer and was raising a brood of children by that time. I could stay with her family as a temporary measure.

If Dan knew I was planning to leave the area, he might let me know when we would be planning our wedding. Imagine my shock when Dan told me he was moving back to Haskell, Oklahoma, to be near his parents. I still didn't know what to think, but we kept corresponding and finally, finally, he proposed in a letter. We agreed to meet in St. Louis. He was to be at a conference there, and that's where he gave me a ring, a beautiful diamond.

But before I could finish the plans to move to Maryland, I got a telephone call from Morsetown High School—that's a small city near Grandview Normal where I had completed the teaching course. I decided to accept the offer of being their nurse at least for the planned year of our engagement. I began the school year elated that I could look forward to "tying the knot." But Dan didn't mention any specific plans, and I began to get uneasy once again. Toward the end of the school year, I felt that I should be forthright with him about Mother. So I wrote and told him about her situation. I felt that if he loved me enough, he would understand and that it wouldn't matter. After all, he was headed for the ministry to be a man of God. I expected that he would be sympathetic and understanding. But he began to write that we should not have children because "insanity runs in families." And suddenly, the letters stopped. I was so distraught— once school ended I took the bus out to Oklahoma to see if there was a chance to repair the damage. We met at his parents' house, and he told me bluntly, "I don't want to get married." Why was I so shocked? He had been dropping hints all along, but there I was, naïve Laura to the core. I tore off the ring and nearly threw it at him.

I found out much later that Irma had played a role in all of this. You see, Dan had come to visit in Norton, to meet the family. And lo and behold, my own sister apparently saw to it that Dan should learn everything. Besides revealing the situation about Mother—he had already learned that from my letter—Irma described Carla's bouts with epilepsy. In later years, I asked her, "Why?" And she said, "I hated our family!" I could understand that—she had given up her first love to take care of everyone. I guess she didn't want anyone else to have happiness. But I couldn't condone her betrayal of me. It took me years to come to terms with this. Over time, she mellowed and we became confidantes by mail, but not until we were in our seventies. Besides, although I couldn't see a clear picture at the time, she had handed me a blessing.

Meanwhile, I had met a teaching colleague at the high school—Mary Ann Welch—who was most interesting, different from the rest of the faculty. She was odd, really quite above most of the other faculty. She was about ten years older and held a master's degree from Stanford. We became friends, and she told me that she had some land in Arizona and coaxed me to go out there with her. I hesitated. I felt lucky to have a good job to be able to support myself and also help with Emma's college expenses. As a school nurse, I tested eyes, removed objects from ears, treated blisters on heels. I also did home visits, which I preferred to teaching subjects in the classroom. I thought, why would I want to live in some God-forsaken desert? But at that point, the breakup with Dan weighed heavily on me. So I finally agreed to give it a try, to test my wings further away from home than I had ever been. I was in hell anyway.

We agreed that neither one of us would quit our jobs, but go out in the summer to Phoenix and give it a try. We headed there the summer of 1929. As it turned out, we managed to make a go of it. It's strange, but if it had not been for Mary Ann, I would not be married to your father. And you and I wouldn't be sitting here talking about all this.

Have I ever told you her story? Pieces of her life came out gradually as we got better acquainted. She trusted me with her secret, and I felt privileged she shared so much about herself. When she was sixteen, she and a boy named Lloyd ran away and got married. She swears that her marriage was not consummated. She didn't want her mother to know—that's why they didn't spend the wedding night together, or get an annulment. At some point, Lloyd decided he didn't want to be married. So they parted. How she managed to keep this secret from her mother, I'll never know. But she did remain technically married to Lloyd although the relationship had ended.

World War I started, and she volunteered to become a nurse. She had all kinds of experiences during the war, traveled to several European cities. She told me that she danced with the Prince of Wales—I wrote a poem about that. She had ambition, so after the war, she went to Stanford, got a degree, sold World Book encyclopedias and made piles of money. She could persuade anyone to do most anything. That's how she convinced your father to marry me!

By the time I met her, she was having some foot trouble, which turned out to be a symptom that her whole body was really breaking down from arthritis. And that's why she wanted to go back to Arizona, to live in a dryer climate. She knew I was recovering from a broken heart, and she asked me go with her.

Now in the East—I learned this at Yale—you didn't go downtown without wearing your white gloves and hat. We arrived in Phoenix on July 4, 1929, in 120-degree weather, but I was still determined to look presentable when I went downtown. Mary Ann and I must have looked like beings from another planet all decked out in our finery, with perspiration pouring down our faces! You would cross your legs and feel perspiration running down them. She had tried to tell me how uncomfortable we'd be but went along with my insistence. She probably smiled to herself—she was quite a card—and figured that I'd learn by letting natural consequences set in.

She found it too hot to stay in the city during the summer, but she had friends in Prescott, which was much cooler. She got me located there doing private duty nursing. Meanwhile, she went off to a nearby Army hospital because her arthritis was getting really bad. I know it because I was afraid to cross the street with her—she was so slow. Anyhow, she came back from that hospital close to being cured.

Since fall was rolling around, we had to decide whether to return to Morsetown. Mary Ann had already been offered a position at a high school in Phoenix. But I hadn't located anything. So I began to telephone all the principals in every school listed in the phone book. There were seven or eight districts. I was about to give up—no job openings for school nurses—but on the last one, the woman principal said she had an opening for a home economics teacher. I told her I had nurse's training, and she seemed interested. What she really wanted to know was if I could teach home economics. I said no and hung up the phone. But I got to thinking about how much I had cooked and sewed, but had no degree in it. I called her right back, and she hired me—to teach seventh and eighth graders.

Once we both knew that we had secure jobs at least for a year, we rented a comfortable apartment with air conditioning to get us through the terrible summer months. It was late in the following summer that the best thing happened—what began the healing I so desperately needed. Your father was a traveling salesman for a paint company. He was living in Los Angeles, but had Phoenix in his sales territory. Apparently, one of his sisters from L.A. had told him to look up a Mary Ann Welch in Phoenix. So he proceeded to go through the phone directory calling every Welch listed. Mary Ann answered the telephone on a day when I was feeling ill with a virus and had taken to my bedroom with a sore throat. Apparently, she said something to the caller like, "I'm not the Mary Ann Welch you are looking for, but I'd like to meet you anyway." And that woman, she gave this man the address to our apartment and invited him over for a cup of tea. Now you would never do that today.

Mary Ann poked her head in and told me—no, she practically ordered me—"Laura, put on your best robe and come out in one hour looking pale and interesting. I have a beau for you."

He knocked at the door and when Mary Ann opened it, there he was—tall and good looking, with wavy brown hair and twinkling blue eyes. As he walked over the threshold, I appeared in a red satin bathrobe, and I don't mind telling you that the sparks flew between us and could have set that robe on fire.

We were engaged within six weeks and got married in October, one day before I turned thirty-one.

I continued to work but had to keep my teaching job a secret because married women in the Depression were not allowed to work, if their husbands had jobs. I kept it all mum and taught for another two years. Finally, when I revealed my marital status to the principal, she was floored. She had to let me go. It was all right. We rented a charming little stone house on Roadrunner Lane and began to await the time when we could learn that we would be starting a family. And I began the most creative time in life—I call them the lyric years—when poetry poured out of me. (*See Appendix for some samples.*)

Another part of my life was fulfilling, too. Now that I was not teaching and because your father earned good money at his sales job, I had time to do some volunteer work in the nursing field. Here's what happened.

Once your father and I settled into married life in Phoenix, we attended a Presbyterian church. I didn't have any problems with it—it wasn't hellfire and brimstone, no predestination. It was kind of middle of the road, you'd say. I went because your father was a Presbyterian. We had tried the Methodist church, but he didn't like to go to the altar for communion. You had to go up to the front in a group and be served. He thought the proper way to do communion was to be at your seat and have the plates of bread and grape juice passed to you by the ushers. You waited for the signal from the minister, drank your juice and ate your little cube of bread, then placed your cup in the little holder on the back of the seat in front of you. He didn't want to get up from his seat. So I became a Presbyterian. How communion was served didn't matter to me.

But I still got that old nagging feeling that I should be serving the Lord. It wasn't that I had raised those fears again, but I felt that I should try to be of service. I hadn't ever acted on that desire to become a medical missionary—the idea that sent me searching for a nursing program. One Sunday at church, we had a guest preacher from a nearby Indian reservation. He talked about how Paul had heard a voice—come over into Macedonia and help us—the message was that we should come and help the Indians.

So I went to the minister and told him I'd like to do some volunteer work, and he referred me to this doctor who went out to a clinic serving the Yaqui Indians. This man needed a driver. Since I was a nurse, I could help him in some other medical tasks too. We went there on certain days and treated them, and I assisted in small ways. Nurses at that time couldn't give shots. This doctor treated lots of trachoma. It's an infection of the eyeballs. I would give him the materials to swab the blisters. And I worked in the kitchen by fixing his meals. There was a Yaqui interpreter who spoke both languages, and this man helped guide the doctor and me so that we could be of some assistance to these people.

The Yaquis had lived in Arizona since the 1800s. They had fled from Mexico because of being persecuted there and camped on the Sonoran desert. One group lived close to Phoenix, and I believe another lived near Tucson. Some had built houses. I helped this doctor for about two years. I stopped doing it around the time that Emma arrived in 1936. But it was an interesting experience. I didn't do it out of guilt. I really did want to be of some usefulness in the community.

From those early years of marriage until about 1975, I settled for the church that your father chose. There were no deep spiritual or religious thoughts for me at that time, certainly not the same level of deep concern that I had as a youngster and teen-ager. I was too busy being a homemaker and mother. By this time, I had distanced myself from that old religion that nearly drove me crazy. I wasn't sure what I believed, but I still felt that it was important to go to church and to enter you in Sunday school. However, we will have to save that story for another time.

Chapter 12

Reflections on Redemption

The idea of redemption appears widely in religion, literature, music, film and politics. Webster's New World Dictionary lists seven meanings for "redeem" [Latin **redimere,** re—back + **edemere**—to get, buy]. In the Christian tradition, redemption most often refers to the attaining of salvation through deliverance from sin; i.e., Christ's sacrifice on the cross. But that is not the only understanding that may accrue to this word. I like to think of my mother's redemption as incorporating three elements of the definitions:

—to set free; ransom; rescue;

—to fulfill, as a promise;

—to make amends for; atone or compensate for.

My mother assumed obligations for caretaking in a family faced with her mother's hospitalization for mental illness. This focus dominated her post-high school life. She lived at home to help out personally and financially. She entered the teaching profession because that is what her sisters had done and what her father insisted that she do. She waited until the youngest sister, Emma, was in high school before addressing her own needs. Duty, sacrifice, noble deeds—all these drove her.

For years, she sought to compensate for, or to make amends for, the loss of a motherly presence in the household. In so doing, she may have been acting the part of redeemer for the younger children. With her quiet and compliant nature, she too often let others dictate the terms of levels of obligations she owed. She easily fell prey to those who made her feel guilty; and to overcome the guilt, she sought to become a perfectionist. Playing the part of the redeemer of others became unhealthy.

Clarity came only later. She could not prevent the consequences of the family tragedy from spilling over into the lives of her siblings, no matter how much effort she made. She alone could not absolve her family from its tainted past. Another way beckoned. When the time came, she began to reflect, to decide and finally, to act. She would follow her star.

The time had come to rescue herself from becoming a permanent fixture in their lives. Instead, she paid attention to that "still, small voice,"[9] the one that whispered, "Listen to your mind and your heart." She summoned her courage when others questioned her choices to sail against the tide. So strong was her drive to fulfill her innate destiny that she forged ahead. By emancipating herself from the family, who had come to depend upon her caretaking of the younger siblings, my mother began to liberate herself. She determined that she would fulfill the promise to herself of becoming trained and educated for work into which she could pour her passions.

In doing so, she took charge, to re-frame —and ultimately redeem—her life.

What lessons did she learn?

By choosing the path to sanity and health, she found redemption in everyday places and in ordinary ways, not specifically in an overt religious context. Indeed, she was discovering that sacrifice—either hers or someone else's—did not necessarily guarantee a successful outcome. She would take responsibility for a limited period of time. But she could not be everyone's caretaker forever.

In every decision lurks a problem. My mother weighed the downside of putting limits on being her sister's keeper. She felt the pull of the family, who questioned her stated desire to leave. Guilt and fear could have taken hold. After all, who would care for her in her needy times? She faced an age-old dilemma, not easily resolved. But in the end, she acted on a piece of paradoxical wisdom: To save your life, you might have to lose it.

---

9   I believe my mother felt that the "still small voice" represented intuition, inner guidance, or conscience. References to "a still small voice" abound in both Eastern and Western literature. My mother was probably familiar with the famous hymn "Dear Lord and Father of Mankind," (1872) by John Greenleaf Whittier. Here is the last stanza: Breathe through the heats of our desire
            Thy coolness and thy balm;
            Let sense be dumb, let flesh retire;
            Speak through the earthquake, wind, and fire,
            O still, small voice of calm.
Whittier takes his idea from the Bible. In I Kings 19:11-12, God sends Elijah the prophet wind, an earthquake, and a fire before finally manifesting himself: "And after the earthquake a fire; but the Lord was not in the fire: and after the fire a still small voice."

Thus, she left behind one life and embarked on a journey to a new one. In the first phase, she entered nurse's training to fulfill a dream begun in childhood. Through this experience, she found true and trusted friendships among her fellow nursing students, a community of women with whom she could bond professionally and personally. With one of these friends she could bare her heart and pour out all the agonies of residual fear of not being ready for the Lord. Secure in the knowledge that someone at last understood her feelings, she began to mend. Another source of redemption emerged as her peers came to admire her academic abilities and sought her out for her talents as an essayist and poet. The nearly mute child and adolescent, riven with fear of failure to be perfect, began to blossom as an attractive and witty woman.

Moving on, she encountered the wild flames of Eros and discovered that love heals. At the point she imagined that her romantic life would evaporate into a series of broken-up relationships, my father magically walked into her life, and they were wed two months later. But her redemption would not be complete without two other things. First, she began to exercise her creative gifts. In her case, it was poetry writing. Some of her best written poems date from these early years of marriage. The other was finding satisfaction in the service to others by assisting a doctor who was offering medical assistance to the Yaqui Indians in Arizona. Here was true service, not sacrifice, the willing hand extended to share one's time and talents by helping others.

By revealing herself to me in the interviews, my mother tapped into a deep vein of feminine wisdom, a treasure trove that has stayed with me. I began to see her life as a testimony to the idea that redemption does not necessarily require the notion of someone's dying to atone for humanity's sins. Instead, the word takes on new meaning. When I thought about this part of my mother's amazing journey, I drew from its story some memorable lessons.

The blessings of luck and good fortune are not sprinkled equally. But whether we are born into poverty or affluence, all of us encounter struggles from which we need to extricate ourselves. No matter what our station in life, we can play a part in our own salvation by looking deep inside and trusting our instincts. All of us possess these inner gifts, which are bestowed by grace, without price. We often fail to recognize these resources because they take the form of the mundane, the ordinary and the commonplace. But these may be unrecognized treasures, lying ready for us to claim. If we recognize their presence, celebrate their mystery and act on their opportunities, we can draw up from the well deep within and satisfy our thirst.

Part Three—Transformation

The way of the Creative works through change and transformation,
so that each thing receives its true nature and destiny and comes
into permanent ... accord with the Great Harmony: this is what
furthers and what ... perseveres.
        —Alexander Pope (1688-1744)

It is slow work to be born again.
        —Henry Ward Beecher (1813-1897)

The heart of a mother is a deep abyss at the bottom
of which you will always find forgiveness.
        —Honore de Balzac (1799-1850)

Chapter 13

Born Again

It is the low ground where the scum and filth of a guilty conscience, caused by the conviction of sin, continually gather, and for this reason it is called the Slough of Despond.
—John Bunyan, *The Pilgrim's Progress*

Through forgiveness, which essentially means recognizing the insubstantiality of the past and following the present moment to be as it is, the miracle of transformation happens not only within but also without.
—Eckhart Tolle, in *The Power of Now: A Guide to Spiritual Enlightenment*

Several years had passed since we had gotten together for more interviews. My life had been disrupted with a number of things, and I just hadn't followed up as well as I should have. Time and events had raced by quickly, and suddenly I realized that my mother was –this is always a shock to an adult child—getting old. Our last three tapes were made in October 1993, a few days before my mother's ninety-fourth birthday. She lived alone now, for my father had passed away in 1991 shortly after I moved to Colorado. He and Mother had been married for sixty-one years. I began traveling to New Mexico to visit her every few months. Although she managed to remain in her home, I could tell that she had aged. She lived alone, slowly becoming increasingly frail and restricted in her ability to carry out necessary household tasks. She engaged a helper three times per week to do errands, help her cook some meals and take her washing to a laundromat. She was fiercely determined to stay put as long as she could. She could no longer take her daily walks, something that saddened me. I could see the physical changes but could still marvel at her sharp mind.

As we talked about the twists and turns of her life, I came back to questions related to how she maneuvered through the shoals of her deeply traumatizing early religious experiences to whatever belief system she had adopted for herself now. Her insights had come gradually, but when they hit, she felt struck by lightning. They had lit up her entire being with a momentous shift of understanding, not only of the mind, but also of something felt deep down—authentic, intuitive, something viscerally real.

Y ou wanted to know how I came to shed the old fears and tremblings about religion from childhood. Well, I'll tell you.

You recall that I was a sleepwalker between ages eight and ten. As I told you, I lived in constant fear of not being ready for the Lord. That feeling persisted in one form or other, off and on, until sometime in high school. Oh, I was happy some of the time, happy that I was doing the Lord's work. But secretly I worried terribly that I wasn't perfect. I was a sinner, I knew it. And I couldn't get over the nagging concern that I wouldn't be ready when the Lord came to take us all up. So I tried to be a perfect person.

I was kind of happy at times. I especially had a great deal of happiness when I was doing what I thought was being right with the Lord. The happiness was only occasional. Most of the time I felt that I wasn't saved.

I can remember saying something about this to Aunt Em—she was a regular old heathen—and she responded, "I believe when we're dead, we're dead and that's all there is to it." Her words shocked me at the time. Another thing—I'm sure I remember hearing her say to Dad that Laura was a lot like Mother, and Dad agreed. And what I didn't understand was that I was filled with anger. But I didn't know it, so instead of finding a way to express my feelings, I would hold it all in. I would get these sensations in my head—things buzzed through my brain. Yes, that's it—my head felt like bees buzzing all around. Can you imagine?

And I developed these compulsions—I thought the Lord was telling me to do this and do that, to hold prayers at the homes of the neighbors, things like that, all of which I told you about, that were against my nature. But I was timid and really didn't want to do things like trying to convert others. Yet I felt that if I didn't, that I was sinning, that I wasn't right with the Lord. All this was before Mother's tragedy happened. After that, everyone else was preoccupied with holding the family together and with moving to Norton. But my head was still somewhere else. I know Dad was concerned that I worried all the time just like Mother. You might think that Mother's tragedy was the cause of my worries, but, honestly, all of these feelings were with me on the farm before Mother's illness came on.

When we got to Norton to be near mother in the mental hospital, we were all taken in as a family to the Methodist church there. Dad arranged it. By this time, I was worse than ever. He noticed how agitated I was most of the time, and he suggested to me that I not go to church for a while. I must have been in a pretty bad state.

I suppose now that I was growing and didn't know it. For right about this time, when I thought I might go as crazy as Mother, several specific crises occurred that led me out of it. Now, I don't mean crises that tear your world apart. I'm talking about the times when your world shifts, when you see things differently, for the better. They were significant stages of my coming to terms with all this religious addiction. You could also call them moments of truth.

The first was when I was seventeen and a junior in high school. I don't remember where I was, but there was this flash—if that's the kind of God he is, I don't want to serve him! And I threw it out—all that religion and what the preachers said, all the "shoulds" and "should nots," and all those fears. Kicked them right out of my system! I knew I was going to hell because I had a lot of anger toward my father—but I said to myself, "There's one thing for sure—he'll be there with me." But you know what? I didn't care! I wasn't rid of the anger, but I had released the fears, killed them completely. I went along after my insight and lived a normal life and didn't worry about sinning. If I was going to the bad place, I might as well have a good time! That's how desperate I was. I knew there was still that trauma down inside of me, but if I hadn't pitched a good bit of it away, I could not have managed my life at all.

The next crisis I remember vividly. I was at Carla's, helping take care of her children. I was not thinking about religion at all when suddenly another flash—a poem that I had memorized from the McGuffey Reader—popped into my mind. It's called "Graditum"—it was written by Josiah Gilbert Holland.[10] The first two verses go like this:

Heaven is not reached by a single bound
But we build the ladder by which we rise
From the lowly earth to the vaulted skies
And we mount to its summit round by round.

I count this thing to be grandly true
That a noble deed is a step toward God
Lifting the soul from the common clod
To a purer air and a broader view.

(This was not the first time during our interviews that my mother recited poetry word for word. I had to marvel how she retained this memory well into her nineties).

I've gotten so many insights from poetry, so when this poem popped into my head, a bombshell hit me. Why, that's all that is required—do noble deeds. Heaven is not reached instantly, but gradually. It's a process and you work toward it. What flashed all over me was that I *wasn't* going to hell. It was one of those "aha" moments. This was my first realization that I was not lost. My long night of despair that I was going to hell evaporated— totally! I didn't think about hell at all from that point on. I wasn't yet what I wanted to be, but the awful burden was gone.

10   Josiah Gilbert Holland lived from 1818-1891. He was founder and editor of *Scribner's Monthly* (later called *Century Magazine*). This poem was published in 1872.

So that's what I call being born again—people see that's
the way things are—insight—seeing through things in a new
way. Another piece of poetry that I like on that same subject is
"When Earth's Last Picture Is Painted," by Rudyard Kipling. The
poem talks about the after-life and how the Master artist will let
each person paint the picture of his life "in his separate star." The
end of the poem says that each person will draw the thing as he
sees it. You see, *if* you have a survival of any kind, or *if* there is an
afterlife, you'll do what you are supposed to do in *this* life. Instead
of trying to do what you think you *ought* to do to make yourself a
place in heaven. And if you do that here and now, while you are
living, I think you *are* saved.

This was different from all those hymns that talk about God
and the way things are after we are gone. And that you have
to be saved, do family prayers, and convert the neighbors. For
so long a time, I had been in fear of death, not being ready for
what came after, not having been pardoned for my sins. But that
moment when I saw clearly—it was terribly liberating. It was
what I call a true conversion—you see it, and it's real. If I *ever*
had a conversion, that was it!

And I know now that conversion isn't this sudden feeling you
get in a meeting or a revival—oh, I'm sure that some do—but
what hit me was that conversion comes in spits and spurts. After
all, what good is a conversion that makes you crazy?

I can't tell you how much I enjoyed being out from that
load. And I couldn't help thinking, what a heavy burden I'd
been carrying all that time. I called it being in the "slough of
despond." [11] Have you read *The Pilgrim's Progress*? The slough of
despond is where he wades through mud and mire—it's all about
describing the progress of a soul to win satisfaction of any kind,
or a new birth, or whatever you call it. Anyway, I'd been going
through that—absolute despair, the period of darkness of the
soul, the slough of despond.

My, what a wonderful feeling! To have a concept of a God
I wasn't afraid of, who wouldn't punish me if I wasn't perfect. I

---

11   In the allegory, Bunyan's hero Christian sinks under the weight of his sins and
his sense of guilt. The "slough of despond" appears in numerous subsequent writings of
Anglo-American literature.

believed there was a God that made the universe, but I finally discarded this idea of a God that would send me to hell if I made one slight mistake. Finally, finally, I began to live a normal life.

There were other influences, too. I remember the professors at Grandview Normal School hooting at the idea of the Bible being historically accurate—Adam and Eve and all that. They called it a fairy story and I did get to the point of doubting somewhat. But I didn't take these misgivings too seriously. I went along doing my teaching until I got to Yale and could talk about it with Marjorie. I lucked out and got a good person. How wonderful to be able to talk to her and have her listen, to tell her things I couldn't tell my sisters or father! We were supposed to be nursing others, and here I was, getting healed. And who knows, with the mother she had, possibly she was, too.

But it wasn't perfect. I still had a lot of anger until later in life when I read *Abundant Living*, by E. Stanley Jones. This is a book of one-page essays on how to lead a fulfilling Christian life. His writings are helpful. They don't make you fearful. They talk about normal problems and how you might solve them in a constructive way by following some of the teachings of Jesus. Your father gave you the last copy we had. I recall that he wrote in the fly leaf, "To my dear daughter in the hope that she will put all these things into practice in her life." I think you were around eight or so.

I remember in one of the chapters, I read, "Be ye angry and sin not." That sentence seemed to be saying something to me— that it was all right to get angry, and I could do that without being labeled a sinner. I was angry with your father for being away from the family, off staking mining claims thinking he could make us rich, instead of working hard at his business and enjoying what we had. Yet I had been trying to see how I could be angry and still be a Christian. That old teaching—that you were a sinner if you showed your anger—I needed to deal with that. So I realized, reading those essays, how twisted my heart had been, and it hit me like a ton of bricks—I needed to forgive him and many others, too.

Now I don't want you to think that this happened all at once, or was finished once and for all. I had to forgive your father innumerable times for driving us into debt and not supporting the family, but each time I forgave him, I felt lighter and happier. The same ideas about forgiveness would return to me over and over again, years apart. So that was another breakthrough.

Along the same lines, I read a book by Catherine Marshall[12] and I came across some lines about the "oughts" and the "any's"—now what on earth did that mean? She then quoted the Lord's Prayer and wrote something like, when you pray, if you have "ought" against "any," well then, forgive. Here was yet another important idea—like that poem about heaven not being reached by a single bound—and I knew that I was still holding hatred.

Of course, there were people I hadn't yet forgiven. This insight struck me as another crisis. I consider it yet another one of my conversions. What swept over me was that I needed to let go of the bitterness I felt towards your father or my father, but also my resentments towards people who had done me wrong. I needed to forgive them, too. The hardest one to forgive—after your father –was Byron Cook, our neighbor in Phoenix who terribly mistreated his wife, Caroline. She was my best friend, and oh, they were so good to us after Emma died. But he cut her down with words all the time, like my father did with me. That man killed her as if he had taken an ax to her, and when we lived there, I couldn't bring myself to forgive him. I had to talk myself into it because Caroline had long ago passed away, of a broken heart, I truly believe. But I did it. I forgave him. Then I started to look back over my life, and if I couldn't find someone, I'd scare up someone. Oh, you can't imagine—I had the biggest, best time forgiving! You know how people feel when they're up the air as they're being converted? I got "high" going about forgiving! I remember waking up each morning, going outside to feed the birds and taking a little walk around the block. And during this

---

12   Catherine Marshall (1914-1983) was married to Peter Marshall, who served as pastor of the New York Avenue Presbyterian Church and Chaplain of the United States Senate. After his death, she began writing, publishing over twenty spiritual and inspirational books.

time, the voice in my mind was going great guns—forgiving all the grudges I still had.

I thought about this woman, the leader of that gang of women from our church—when you were little—they were so nasty to me and excluded me from their "friendship" circle. I had felt so hurt, but you know what I did? I invited them all over to our house, made a lovely cake and served them tea. I looked into the eyes of the one I knew was the ringleader, the one who whispered behind my back. And I stared her down with my brightest, broadest smile! Well, what could she do? If I didn't let her hurt me, I think that means I managed to forgive her.

I began to forgive ridiculous things and sad things. On winter mornings, when I'd go out on the porch to get the milk, I used to get annoyed that the milkman put the bottles there so early that the cream would freeze. Now isn't that silly? So I forgave the milkman. I loved to feed the birds, and there was this cat hanging around ready to pounce on them. So I forgave the cat for trying to kill them, and I left some milk for it in a saucer. I forgave whoever stole your doll buggy and the girls that offered you candy but instead drove pins into your palm. First I'd laugh at myself, and other times I felt like crying.

I forgave my mother for trying to kill herself and leaving us to keep the family going and causing all the trauma we later suffered, and I forgave my sisters and brother for not believing me about Emma's suicide. I forgave Dad for killing our cat, and the maid who stole my ruby ring at Yale, and Irma for breaking up my engagement to Dan, and Emma for taking her own life. And yes, hard as it was, I forgave Henry Michael Delaney—my father—for all his insults and sarcasm and stinginess. All these grievances that I had stored up for years—I let them all out like air out of a balloon. I didn't have anyone to talk to now, not since Marjorie and I had those conversations back in nurse's training. So I wrote letters and tore them up, I wrote poetry, I sang hymns to myself. Once I started letting go of all the grudges I had kept close, I could now finally wave them goodbye.

But I didn't think about forgiving myself—not until you mentioned it after I told you about Emma. Once after we had that talk, the one where we sat out on the back patio and watched the sunset, I took a little walk one spring morning down to a neighborhood park. The flowers were all budding out, and their scents were lovely. Suddenly I saw at my feet a sprouting of Queen Anne's Lace, the first of the season. Someone whom I've long forgotten from the farm days once told me why he thought spring was best of all seasons —"because that's when we get un-sewed from our winter clothes." Where I grew up, the coming of the first spear of Queen Anne's Lace and the first dandelion shoot signal the occurrence of that ecstatic feeling of coming "un-sewed."

That brought back all those memories of early spring in the hill country. That morning on my walk, I remembered springtime in my early years, those carefree times before all the worry and religious fears nearly brought me down. And that phrase about getting "un-sewed" from our winter clothes" came back to me as if it were yesterday. It was time to let the seams out of the fabric of my wintry heart and release the last of all the anger and guilt and pardon myself for not being perfect. Because here was so much beauty right here under my feet, right now in our Southwestern spring, even as it reminded me of the long ago time in the country, in which there had been so much overlooked ecstasy.

That moment of past and present blending—it was the best conversion of all. I was so engrossed in my own thoughts that I didn't notice a passerby until she approached me and asked a bit rudely, "Whatever are you doing by picking the flowers here?" Apparently, while forgiving everyone in my head, I was not aware that I had stooped down and snapped off a sprig of Queen Anne's lace. She startled me so, that I dropped the flower, smiled at her and said, "Oh, I've been thinking about what a wonderful morning it is. Isn't it?

Chapter 14

A Dialogue on Faith: Beginning

*Ask, and it will be given you; Seek, and you will find; Knock, and
it will be opened to you.*
—Jesus (Luke 11:9)

*Her voice was weaker now, with periodic crackles. She repeated
some stories but never changed the essential facts of the narrative.
Early on, I had seen my role as one of extracting information. I was
the questioner; she was the responder. But in these latter days, we had
settled into a comfortable rapport with each other. Our relationship
had undergone a subtle shift, and we found ourselves conversing as
two intimate friends. Now our attention shifted to discussions of her
long saga of steps to reconcile her religious past.*

*Up to this point, I had let my mother's voice carry the story of
her life. My comments and reactions came forth as brief responses
to her central narrative. As the interview project neared its end, we
became collaborators in sharing the stories of our separate but similar
spiritual quests. I came to see that in these last interchanges we had
showed signs of mending those mother-daughter wounds that had
brought about the tape project in the first place. In the beginning, we
had formed two parallel, somewhat icy streams that finally melted and
flowed together as one body of water.*

*What follows are excerpts of these interchanges in which we both
contributed our thoughts. The topics centered on her growth and
change in matters of religion and spirituality, as well as my own
spiritual development. We also veered off into musings about our
personalities and our pasts, both of which held echoes of similar father-
daughter relationships. Our give and take felt much different from the
earlier recorded interviews. In some ways, they remain in my heart as
the most enriching of all our conversations.*

Nancy Key Roeder

NANCY—You were exposed to a certain type of religion, and it affected you differently from your other sisters because of your personality. I kept remembering how often you referred to the impact of fear-based religion. Recently I attended a workshop at a retreat called "Healing the Religious Wounds of the Past." In my church, many of the members came from the same sort of strict, inhibiting kinds of religion that you were exposed to, leading them to feel there was no need to have any religion or God. But they got stuck in a rebellious stage, and the whole idea of this workshop was to realize that their rebellion was not healthy, either. Now I don't want you to think that I have any religious wounds—you were wonderful in protecting me from the same kind of thing you went through—but I signed up for the workshop because I was interested in understanding what some of the others had gone through and how their experiences would compare and contrast with yours.

MOTHER—I'm sure I am not the only one who ever went through this. It may have seemed that way, out on an isolated farm with no one comprehending what I was feeling.

NANCY—I've heard your stories about your fears and worries and how you kicked religion out of your life, how you got rid of your anger through forgiving those who "trespassed against you." I got the impression that in your married life you went to whatever church Dad chose because you thought it was the right thing to do in our family. I'm thankful that both you and Dad sought churches that would present a loving God to me. That's what I remember from childhood—nothing like what you went through. Is that right?

MOTHER—Yes, it's exactly as you say it. That was my history. I was determined you wouldn't have to suffer the same way I did. Your dad didn't argue with me about that one.

NANCY—So I thought it might be good to do some interviews that bring us up to date—where are you now? I know

188

that you must have changed since I left home in 1960. I'd really like to know where things are now for you. Would that be all right? And if you have a pause, is it all right to ask you follow-up questions?

MOTHER—Yes, I wish you would ask me questions because it helps me to get a focus.

NANCY—I remember that your concept of God was this authoritarian, powerful person that was going to wreak havoc on you if you made one misstep.

MOTHER—He was a policeman.

NANCY—And when you did the things you were told that you should do, it was against your own nature. You tried to conform, do what you thought you should do, even if it didn't fit you temperamentally.

MOTHER—Yes, and it threw me off balance mentally and emotionally.

NANCY—But recently you said that you now felt that you were in relationship with God—that He is present in your life. Can you expand on that?

MOTHER—It began shortly after that crisis I told you about after reading the book by Catherine Marshall, the passage about forgiveness. It slowly dawned on me that there was a presence, or something you could call a relationship—that the Lord was present all the time, that he wasn't away off there. It took me some time to absorb this idea, but I really felt it. It was as if I had found God after throwing Him out of my life.

NANCY—Or, do you suppose that because you started forgiving people, God found you?

MOTHER—That's a good way to put it.

NANCY—I was so grateful to you that you didn't put me through the same kind of experience.

MOTHER—I did try to shield you. Why don't you tell me what your earliest memories were?

(This was the first time that Mother deviated from trying to answer my questions by turning the tables on me. Suddenly, the dynamics shifted, and I became the one being interviewed.)

NANCY—Pretty hazy, but overall I think they were of a loving God. I didn't get fearful. I do remember when I was around five and we were living in that small town south of Albuquerque, that we went to a community church, but I don't remember the style except that there was no shouting. I also know that Dad was getting obsessed about being superintendent of the Sunday school.

MOTHER—He only got interested in church when he could do something like that, be the big cheese and be recognized.

NANCY—Anyhow, the first negative thing I recall—I was around six—was of running up and down the steps of the church, outside. And you took me aside and said, "You can't do that because you will get criticized."

I loved new words. So I asked you about that one. "*Criticized?* What does that mean and how do you spell it?"

I now know there was a lot of social control, and that your peer group of women would chitchat behind your back—you felt bad about it—I take it you weren't really fond of that church.

MOTHER—It was the people in it—it was the feeling of—a lot of cliquishness. I didn't belong to the clique, the Friendship Society. I thought that was the worst misnomer. I wasn't taken into the group as I felt that I should be. It related partly to criticism of you.

NANCY—I know, I realize that. Why? Because I was so active?

MOTHER—You were quite curious, but I think it was pretty normal at that age to want to work off some steam by jumping up and down the church steps. I mean, I didn't want to put you in a strait jacket!

NANCY—Didn't they have little children, too?

MOTHER—It wouldn't have mattered. They were doing it to pull me down, that's all. They didn't see me as part of their social class—they were mostly railroad people.

NANCY—What else did I do that offended them?

MOTHER—They saw that you whispered in church, or something like that. You asked questions about the sermon and the hymns, what did those words mean and so forth. You can tell when a group gossips or talks to one another—one of them separately treats you the same way that the other one has, so you understand they've been together, if you know what I mean. Anyway, that's the feeling I got. In time, I learned it roundabout from one member. This other member—I think her Christian conscience got to her—finally broke down and told me what the criticism was. Well, that kind of turned it around. Now that I knew why they were excluding me, I went to another member that I felt I could trust and told her how hurt I was about this, and she was tactful enough to smooth it over, so that I finally got absorbed into their Friendship Circle some way. And for whatever happened, I've told you that I've forgiven all that.

NANCY—I remember when we moved in that town to the Hispanic neighborhood where everyone was Catholic, but we were Protestant. And some of the neighborhood boys would throw rocks at me in the back yard. There was a lot of resentment because we were Anglos. And you would bake cookies and take them over to their mothers. I didn't realize at the time the great way that you disarmed them and still protected me.

MOTHER—(*laughs*)—Do you remember how you begged to go to the Catholic Church and see your neighborhood friends' First Holy Communion?

NANCY—Yes, that was the drama to end all dramas! I longed to be part of the Catholic Church. We didn't have anything like that for the girls in our church. They were dressed in beautiful white dresses and were going through this gorgeous ritual with candles, and it was obvious to me that whole tribe felt this was important. I suppose if I missed anything, that was it—our church had no recognition that passages and recognition were important for kids, and no particular way to single out kids and make us feel special in some way. I thought this was the greatest show on earth and wondered why I couldn't have a First Holy Communion.

MOTHER—I figured that some of this longing was due to the fact that your father didn't pay enough attention to you.

NANCY—I know that certainly was a piece of it.

MOTHER—You had one terrible experience. Do you remember it?

NANCY—I think you might be referring to the only other Anglo family a couple of blocks away. She was a local preacher's daughter, wasn't she? Yes, you finally let me go to one service at her father's church, where he nearly scared me to death. I remember the sermon as mostly screaming, over and over, "Repent and be saved!"

MOTHER—You came home all shaken up and asked me, "Mother, am I saved?" As you can imagine, I didn't want you to go through a re-run of my life, so I shot back. "You know what? You were never lost!" That ended that, and you didn't go back.

NANCY—I certainly didn't retain any emotional scars from that one-time experience. I guess it was beginning to sink in that people had all kinds of different ways of doing religion. Possibly the seeds were planted for how I managed to work things out in my own mind.

MOTHER—Do you remember your prayers?

NANCY—Yes, I think they all reinforced being a good girl, and later on, I had to unlearn how to be a good girl. It was difficult to defend myself from aggressive people. I somehow had gotten the idea that if you were polite to people, they would treat you fairly. It took me a long time to learn to stand up for my rights. But that was the prevailing way of teaching children— there's nothing for you to feel guilty about. I don't think I was in any way traumatized by saying my prayers at night.

MOTHER—Is that the way you felt in junior high and high school?

NANCY—I don't remember thinking deeply about theology or God or anything like that. Church was important, but the social community was the big thing. I recited all the required creeds and so forth in church but didn't stop to question their meaning. I think early on, I learned that as a girl and a Christian, I wasn't supposed to express any doubts or questions. Just accept. And it was easy for me to memorize. So why not go with the flow? The church services were beautiful with the choir coming up the aisle and candles being lit. And the sermons were down to earth about how to live our lives. Practical stuff. You could get some ideas on how to be moral and how to love your neighbor. So things remained at that level until I got to the university.

MOTHER—What happened to change you? I know you go to a liberal church right now.

NANCY—I struggled with my upbringing and the things I'd been taught were true. I did a great deal of thinking and reading about all of it. What kept bothering me was that if God was so loving and caring, which I had been taught, then why wasn't I getting that kind of treatment from my own father? If there was a Father-God, for sure my Dad was not the expression of this kind of God or any form of it. He was so distant, not at all interested in what I was doing and accomplishing at school. When I faced up to the reality that he didn't care—that acceptance led me to question the meaning of God. There was this discrepancy between the way God was described in church and Dad's actions. Oh, I know, he wasn't abusive or alcoholic or anything like that, but he seemed to care only about himself, not about you or me or our family. He didn't know when my birthday was, and he didn't bother to come to my high school graduation. But, oh, did he make sure I got to church. Oh well, I'm getting off track here.

MOTHER—You don't know how much heartbreak I had over this. He was definitely all wrapped up in himself.

NANCY—Why is it we measure our concept of God against our relationship with our fathers? Both you and I did this. I had not known about the difficult relationship you had with your father until we made these tapes, but there are some parallel experiences.

MOTHER—So what happened to your faith after you went to college?

NANCY—Ultimately, I discarded the idea of God as a "personal God" and as a male—I don't think God *is* a male. I came to think of God as a combination of male and female traits, and that—if there is a God—he/she would be everything that exists. And I realized—but this was much later—what a trip was done on women to assume that it's a "he." All that language is filled with "Father God," "Father, Son and Holy Ghost"—all male. There are other religions prior to Christianity that created female goddesses and it took me a lot of years of reading and sorting things out.

MOTHER—Oh, I never thought of that—the thing about the language referring only to men—

NANCY—Other insights that came to me a couple of years ago after reading tons of material on addictions—was that Dad possibly was a religious addict. He was using his religion as a substitute to put distance between people in close relationships in the same way that other people put alcohol, drugs, hobbies or whatever between themselves and those who care for them. I just finished a book on religious addiction that helped me see this.

MOTHER—Yes, he had an addictive personality, and I realize it did cause real dysfunction in our family.

NANCY—Getting back to your question about how I changed my ideas on religion, I finally came to join a progressive church that believes there are truths in lots of religions. I came to feel that God was not a person, a personality, but the all-powerful creative force in the universe. And whatever it is, it would not make us limit ourselves if our minds, bodies and spirits took us away from a really narrow view—that was *my* conversion.

MOTHER—I'm relieved that you didn't have the scars that I had over religion.

NANCY—I don't have any kind of religious wounding such as you got full blown. The fact that you allowed me to come to my own conclusions was the best thing that you could have done! I could add that my father's lack of closeness and attention helped this process—because in some ironic way, it freed me to seek other paths.

MOTHER—You think so?

NANCY—Yes, absolutely. You gave me a structure at the appropriate child development stages. Of course, I did have to work through some things. The way children were raised at that time—you had to be a good girl because that is what is expected.

Boys can act out but girls can't. That's the way nearly every mother raised her children—it wasn't unique to you! That's how it was. I don't carry resentment or anything.

MOTHER—I'm really grateful for what you have told me. How about your university experiences?

NANCY—I was growing intellectually. I was trying to figure out why so much of what I'd learned in Sunday school and church—the literal interpretation of the Bible—didn't make any sense. And yet numbers of my friends believed in it. I felt that religion had some important statements, but things like ... it doesn't seem possible that there was a virgin birth. And how could a body really come alive again—how do you explain the resurrection? And I was a bit anxious. I wondered, did those questions make me a heathen?

MOTHER—I'll tell you my views on the virgin birth later— and you might be surprised. For now, I want to hear what you have to say about how you grew and changed.

NANCY—The serious problem for me was dealing with Dad—he totally ignored me in high school. Except when I accidentally left a book by Faulkner sitting around and he picked it up and read a few passages. He told me it was evil and I shouldn't read things like that. And he didn't want me to be in the senior play because anyone in drama was definitely immoral. And he wanted me to get down on my knees and confess my sins to Jesus Christ. Really radical things like that.

(Mother's voice began to sound weary and a bit bitter—I knew these things were painful for her to hear, especially to recognize at this age. I bit my lip and started apologizing. Should I have brought up these subjects?)

MOTHER—My ego is affected, and I regret that I didn't stand up to your father.

NANCY—To my mind, it was *your* efforts that helped our family to be not as crazy as it could have been, that prevented us from having a total breakdown. I understand that entirely and totally appreciate your efforts. I don't want you to forget that. Most women of your generation—and mine, too—were taught that submissive role. From what I've read, everyone who begins to understand how addiction works in families looks back and sees how they contributed to the dysfunction. You do it unconsciously.

I think the worth of these insights is to help stop future generations from getting into the same kind of cycle.

MOTHER—I've read some things, too—and I realize I was an enabler. You can be submerged in another person's personality and unintentionally encourage them in their addiction. I can see that I was an enabler all my life, that I had been an enabler for the rest of the family. And they saw it and took advantage of me.

NANCY—You mentioned that they let you cook all of the food for your mother, when you took her picnic lunches on Sundays.

MOTHER—They assumed I would do it. When Gretchen and Frieda went to take those summer courses, they took it for granted that I would take care of Margaret and Emma. On the farm, Mother was trying to get some things at the market to drop at the schoolhouse. And who would speak up but Laura? I was so eager to please, and said, "I'll do it." Another example—when Emma wanted to be baptized by immersion, the others didn't pay attention to what she wanted. So I took her and took care of all that. I think that in the way I took pains to follow others' wishes, I might have been a masochist!

NANCY—Yes, by making it possible to meet their needs but not your own. That's how you feed the addiction.

MOTHER—I guess I've been an enabler all my life.

NANCY—There's a question as to the role that birth order, inborn traits, environment play in all of this. No one knows.

MOTHER—I think I was a psychopathic personality—a person who didn't react to life the same way as others –a little bit weird.

NANCY—I disagree, I don't think you were a psychopathic personality. I think you had a sensitive temperament that internalized things in a deeper way than your siblings and friends. And you were so intelligent. There are plenty of brilliant people who can't handle things around them. Look at the artists and musicians who have personal troubles. We don't know how much we are shaped by circumstance and what is inborn. And there are brain chemicals and traumatic experiences. It's quite the brew.

MOTHER—Do you realize what kept me from going insane? It was the fact that I had intelligence. If I had not, I don't think I would have had the sense to throw off this stuff. That's what saved my mind.

NANCY—You certainly were intelligent. And I think that played into your decision to take responsibility for your mental health. You did it! And, when you threw off all that heavy sack of sin—what you had been told was sin—by golly, the heavens didn't open up and a lightning bolt didn't come down and strike you dead!

(Lots of laughter)

MOTHER—The sky didn't fall at all—that was the beginning of the trip to heal my mental state.

NANCY—You'd had enough—you drew a psychic line in the sand and said to yourself, "I'm not going to be in pain any longer. This hurts. I don't like it. And I'm not going to continue to suffer like this." For whatever reason and by whatever mechanism, you saved yourself—that was a demarcation in which in you began to feel that you were a worthwhile human being and weren't going to be beaten down by that kind of religion. You took action instead of someone leading you around by the nose—

MOTHER—That's interesting—complimentary.

NANCY—Let's go back to this idea of being in relationship with God. Tell me more about that.

MOTHER—I don't know, from the point I started forgiving people, it seemed as if I now had a relationship with the real God, that He was present with me all the time. You see, if I forgave them, I knew that He forgave me for anything I might have done or felt in the past. That's a different feeling than anything I'd ever had about religion—that God is closer, not away off there.

NANCY—I know you were in a church in California, when we both lived in the San Diego area in the 1970s.

MOTHER—Oh yes, that experience really continued reinforcing me—that was my first introduction to a charismatic church.

NANCY—I remember knowing that the 1970s saw the birth—or at least the flowering—of the charismatic movement in all faiths.

MOTHER—Yes, it blossomed forth. It started a long time ago before I was born with the Shouting Methodists—but the modern element of it is quite different. The minister in the church in California was one of the most significant things in both of our lives. He was so understanding—he had a gift for communication, to talk and express his belief and his feeling and his concern for you. He was a great influence, and we both loved him.

NANCY—So what was the message? Obviously, not like what you heard in your childhood.

MOTHER—*Nothing* like that! These charismatics are not the least bit fond of religiosity. No, they are concerned with having a relationship, with believing that God is right there with you. So that's the message. As I said, what I heard reinforced where I already was. It wasn't that I first encountered the idea in these churches.

NANCY—That's an important message.

MOTHER—Oh, it is! That's the reason we sought out that kind of church when we moved back to Albuquerque. This kind of religion appealed to your father more than the Presbyterian Church that he had been raised in. But he and I had different reasons and responses. It was good we both got something out of it.

NANCY—So you located a church here?

MOTHER—The pastor was similar in character to the minister we liked so much in California. People like that radiate love and concern for you. I feel like I have had a lot of growth since my conversion about forgiving people. That all happened before we found the church, but they are truly into this forgiveness business—they insist on its importance.

They may be fundamentalists in some things, but they are not fundamentalists in their actions, in their living the things they believe in, and in their sermons telling us how to associate with one another. It's interesting that they keep saying in nearly all of their sermons that if you're failing in your spiritual life, you might have unforgiveness in your heart, and you need to dig down and see if there's someone you haven't forgiven. Yes, I had discovered that earlier, and they are absolutely right.

Chapter 15

A Dialogue on Faith: Continuing

> *We are not human beings having a spiritual experience.*
> *We are spiritual beings having a human experience.*
> —Pierre Teilhard de Chardin

We took a break for supper. On this visit, I was staying with friends who had given me the run of their kitchen, so I had brought over some soup and put together a salad. As always, Mother provided her home baked bread. It was no longer from her oven. She now supplied the recipe to a local baker. Tasks performed with ease all her life were now becoming increasingly difficult for her.

It seemed so long ago, back in California, when she came to my house on the hillside, where we drank tea from her hand-painted cups and felt the breeze wafting through the flowing drapes. But now, the late October night was too chilly, and she was too weary to step outside. We seated ourselves in the living room on a rust sateen sofa beneath an oil painting of a gray weathered farmhouse, and I turned on the tape recorder for what turned out to be our last interview together.

NANCY—This afternoon, earlier, you said something about wanting to delineate the things you either weren't sure about or about which you differed from the beliefs in your church. And you thought I wondered how you could think so differently and still like the church. Could you talk about those things now?

MOTHER—I remember, yes.

NANCY—All right, my question is—knowing you want to be in this church—what are you not sure of, or what points do you disagree with?

MOTHER—To begin with, I like the church because of the people and the caring, the love that's in it. If they made me say that I believe in some of things they talk about, oh, I couldn't have joined. But it happens to be the type of church that is—flexible—a good deal like the congregation and church that you belong to.

Under the current pastor—it's possible another minister might be different—you could believe anything. Now they did assume that you had made Christ your savior and a few things like that, but you didn't have to say it. You just had to sign a membership card. I was able to join without making any stiff promises. And I can listen to some of that and keep my own counsel. If it goes against what my feelings truly are, I simply listen and take in what helps me. That's how I can stay in this church.

If I came out of the closet to the congregation with some of my beliefs, I'd be called a heretic!

NANCY—Yes, you mentioned you'd tell me about your beliefs about the virgin birth.

MOTHER—I have problems with it.

NANCY—There are lots of virgin birth stories in other cultures. I think they arise because they explain something mysterious and endow a particular leader with special qualities.

MOTHER—I know that, and I know that much of what is written in the gospels—a lot of it is rumor. The only one that tells of that is Luke. Have you read the beginning of Luke? He says that this is to inform you of all the stories that have been going around. Luke was a doctor, he was educated. It has been found in examining his work that he was a good historian. He says that he doesn't state facts but stories that have been told. As any historian will write, in order to learn these things that he put forth in his gospel, he must have gone around and talked to people. Now who would tell him something like that except

Mary? He went and talked to Mary. What was that Mark Twain said? I think he wrote that Mary fooled around with other people and made up this story to tell Joseph! Twain was sacrilegious. But it's my private opinion that he was onto something. I can believe his explanation, even if he might have been joking about how Mary got pregnant.

(We both laugh till the tears run down our faces.)

NANCY—To me, that's not the central thing—how the sperm and the egg got fertilized, but the interpretation that people put on it and the resulting belief that the created child is miraculous or magic.

MOTHER—Mary is the one who perpetuated it. Luke reports what she said to the angel and how the angel came to her and to Joseph. So I take all that—

NANCY—You're right that you couldn't be forthright with these views—

MOTHER—Another thing, when the apostles began to believe it was a virgin birth, they had some explaining to do as to how Jesus was in the line of Joseph. They say he is in the line of Joseph. Matthew brings the line of David on down to Joseph, and Mary says about her son Jesus, "who was thought the son of Joseph." Well, how, if he was supposed to be the seed of David, could he not have actually been the son of Joseph?

When our California pastor visited here—he had been reared a Catholic—I asked him. I said, "The Bible teaches that Jesus was of the line of David. Was Mary from the line of David? Because if she wasn't, how could Jesus be from the line of David if it was a virgin birth and he wasn't Joseph's son?" He kind of bowed out of that one, said there were some things he didn't believe in. I guess that's the reason he jumped over from being a Catholic.

NANCY—I do not think that respected scholars in the major religions—including Catholic scholars—push the idea of a literal virgin birth. I could be wrong about this. But I think there might be a wide gap between what theologians and regular churchgoers believe.

MOTHER—I have read a couple of books on the Dead Sea Scrolls. And some on the prophecies that show how they are fulfilled. There was one about the Easter deception which I think went too far in saying that these prophecies were made about Jesus and he went about fulfilling them. But it made a good point. There are some of the prophecies that sound pretty fishy. For example, in the scrolls they found translations of the book of Isaiah and prophecies that Isaiah made, but Jesus couldn't have fulfilled all of these on his own volition—I keep an open mind there. I know Jesus was familiar with Jewish history and sacred writings, so he might have believed he was fulfilling those prophecies. But people misinterpret and turn the thing around, saying that the earlier writings predicted all the things that Jesus was and did.

Going back to this prophecy about the virgin birth—the Living Bible has a different version in that place in Isaiah where it says that a virgin shall be with child—it isn't talking about prophesying that a virgin will have a child—"virgin" is a young girl—Some of the explanations that make sense to me are that this passage doesn't refer to something that was going to happen. Instead, it referred to the young girl, a wife of Isaiah the prophet, that she was going to have a child.

NANCY—That's it—you have to look at the language to see what was meant. We don't have the original texts, but translations and copies by hand. Mistakes could have been made.

MOTHER—But you have to settle for what you have faith in, take it on faith, and let go of what you don't feel comfortable with.

NANCY—That's absolutely right, keep searching for what makes sense to you—

MOTHER—One reason I don't discuss these things with people—anyone but you—it would disturb them a lot if I told them some of my beliefs. Once I shared my beliefs—and this was back in Phoenix—with Caroline, who was devout and avid about her faith. You can tell that some of these ideas aren't exactly new with me. But these ideas distressed her so that she came close to crying. So I decided that I wouldn't hurt anyone ever again.

NANCY—Especially when they hold these beliefs strongly, they feel it's a real threat to them.

MOTHER—But those are the two basic things—you are not supposed to be called a Christian unless you believe in the resurrection and the virgin birth.

NANCY—What is your view of the resurrection?

MOTHER—I keep an open mind on it. If God is a spirit, well, it could have happened. I don't know, I'm mostly persuaded that it could have happened—there's a power somewhere—and there's so much evidence that the body was never recovered. Now there could be an explanation, but I can't help but believe that some way it would have been found. Somebody would have found it—the disciples couldn't have done it, but the Romans could have. Nobody but the Romans could have taken that body and disappeared with it. The disciples couldn't have gotten it because it was guarded by the Romans. And you know that the disciples believed it. They weren't trying to pull a hoax on people, because they would have died, been thrown to the lions and drawn and quartered for holding that belief that he was resurrected. So I don't know—I'm leaving that up to someone else to discover someday.

NANCY—There are definitely some puzzling circumstances. Again, it's one of those things that—I don't think it's going to be a major factor in how much depth of spirituality you have.

MOTHER—No, I agree with that.

NANCY—If it truly did happen, it is probably explained by phenomena that we can't yet understand. These things were reported thirty to sixty years after they supposedly happened. What is important for me was what Jesus said, and the way he lived and the things he taught. These were so powerful that they affected the course of history.

In my mind—and I'm not telling you what to believe because this is my own take—the resurrection falls in the category of the virgin birth. Not that these stories aren't important, but they are not the defining factor as to how we find ourselves now. I find meaning in the stories we know about Jesus' life and teaching and how they can help with the challenges in our lives.

MOTHER—I think that's the most important thing.

NANCY—There are plenty of mainstream Christians who have different interpretations. Scholars and others try to understand what the original language was saying and also what the meaning was for those who experienced it. I mean, I suppose the mystery and awe swirling around Mary was a way to ... well, if you have some kind of special event that supposedly defies nature, there's the "proof" that this person truly is divine or whatever.

MOTHER—Yes, that he was who he said he was. And Jesus himself never said anything, about being born of a virgin!

NANCY—You could ask yourself, what is the meaning of his message? He told us the ways that we need to live. That, to me, is powerful, more so than how or when or where he was born.

As for the resurrection story, it had a special meaning to people in another historical time. And the story was circulated to prove this person was special. There are supposedly eyewitnesses, but everything recorded was way after Jesus' death and told from hearsay. Maybe there was a literal resurrection, we don't know. There's lots of mystery about matter and energy. But if it really did happen, what does that signify? What does it mean for us in our historical time? And if it didn't happen, does that diminish the importance of one of the primary messages of Christianity, which is about loving your neighbor and doing right by others? Oh, I know some people feel that to be a Christian you have to be "saved," and they think that Jesus died for everyone's sins. But to me, it's about ethics and relationships and having peace in your heart. I don't see this resurrection thing as having much to do with inner spirituality.

And I wonder, too—if you "buy" that someone washes away your sins, doesn't that eliminate your sense of responsibility for your own actions? It may be a comforting thought, but how realistic?

MOTHER—Yes, what it means to us is what matters. The gospel of Mark was written thirty years after Jesus' death.

NANCY—That's still a long time.

MOTHER—Oh, I don't know. Thirty years isn't much. If something happened like that, someone being raised from the dead, wouldn't you remember that?

NANCY—Yes, but that length of time does a lot to memory. I could not recall all the details of things that happened thirty years ago, but something memorable, profound, incredible—yes, the essence of it would stay.

MOTHER—That's what I'm saying.

(Here, my skepticism and my mother's belief system started to separate. But we continued to talk in the most congenial manner.)

NANCY—But I'm saying that the people that Mark interviewed would be hard pressed to remember the literal details precisely.

MOTHER—What I was starting to say was that some of the words of Jesus were absolutely not recorded accurately because there was no shorthand to take it down. But as you say, the core remains.

NANCY—The gospel writers all record the details slightly differently in the four different gospels.

MOTHER—And these things—the virgin birth and literal resurrection—they are not that important in developing a relationship with God.

NANCY—I totally agree.

MOTHER—I mean, Jesus typified the good things that God wanted to give to the human race. And couldn't he give them to you by letting the child be born in a regular human way? To me, it doesn't matter. As a matter of fact, I think that was manufactured afterward. I don't think Jesus believed it himself! I think his followers made it up to deify him. If Jesus had been, he would have said something about it.

NANCY—I'm amazed at how much we agree upon! And here, I don't attend a Christian church.

(Once again, my mother's words utterly astounded me. She seemed to be affirming a universal outlook on theology but taking only the ideas most important to her to illuminate her own religious life. And here she was in the midst of people who would be horrified if they knew her views!)

MOTHER—Okay, there's another thing that I can't go along with in my church. They think if you speak in tongues you get the baptism of the Holy Spirit, because of the account in Acts. I don't know what happens in this. I do know that they get a palaver going—it doesn't sound like babble, it sounds rather pretty—now how it happens, I don't know.

NANCY—I think it's an altered state of consciousness. I think they whip themselves into an irrational mental state. And I think that it's perfectly possible to do that—but I think it's all explainable, too.

MOTHER—Another thing, this idea of "being slain in the spirit." I've seen these things happen. These people fall over, straight down on the floor in a group when touched by this healer—is it hypnotism, or what is it? It happens with so-called faith healers when the evangelist lays their hands on them.

NANCY—I've come to think of that as mass hypnosis.

MOTHER—These people believe that it's the power of God.

NANCY—The way I think about it is something of an altered state—you know, the yogis walking on coals—it is possible to have that much mind control.

MOTHER—I guess that's possible.

NANCY—I know they believe that, but I'm sure that there's a rational explanation consistent with human experience and knowledge. There are actually pressure points on the body, and if you are touched in the right places, you lose muscle control. This is well known in Oriental medicine, and this technique is used as the basis for some of the martial arts—how to protect yourself and disarm your enemy.

MOTHER—They call it being slain in the spirit. I don't know what it is, but I know it happens. Same thing about the tongues. But I can't accept it—I just can't! Call me irreligious—

NANCY—Remember what you said about what's important to you about this church—the loving people and your relationship with God.

MOTHER—Yes, of course. But I did want to tell you that I definitely believe in the power of healing by the mind—that's part of my whole experience, how I used my mind to go in the direction of healing instead of the way my mother went. You believe in that, too, don't you?

NANCY—Loosely, with some interpretation as to the context.

MOTHER—And here's another thing that isn't as important—whether we're saved or not. What's critical is that we're in tune with the universe. I call it making friends with the universe.

NANCY—Wow! Those are phrases we use in my church— being in tune with the universe.

MOTHER—I think I could have been any religion that preached love and getting along with your neighbor. I could have been a Buddhist or a Jew or I don't know what all. But since I was raised a Christian and now have come to re-define it, I feel comfortable with things as they are now.

NANCY—That's totally understandable.

MOTHER—Here's another thing—the atonement—that Jesus atoned for our sins. I think of that figuratively, that he lived in such a way to show us what sin was and how to get rid of it. I can believe in the concept of atonement, but not exactly the way it's expressed.

NANCY—Here's how I feel about that. I think it's a common story of scapegoating and sacrifice. It goes way back. The Aztecs did it by taking a man up the stairs and cutting out his heart. Abraham was supposed to sacrifice his first-born son to God. And he used a lamb instead. Apparently, Christianity made a real breakthrough and transformed all this. After Jesus suffered and died on the cross, the story evolved that one person had borne the sacrifice, and no one else needed to do it in that bloody way. All of that to me goes back to something in our primal brain, back to our primitive and barbaric past. In Christianity, things got sanitized—it's so powerful and nice to say that somebody took care of all the rottenness we do—

MOTHER (*nodding*)—Yes, I see what you mean. That you don't need any further sacrifice—that the one sacrifice now and for all puts an end to a lot of those bloody sacrifices that were required.

NANCY—Another part of it is that there is a powerful human need to appease the gods and bargain with them in exchange for not smiting us down. But I don't buy that we need a scapegoat for the depravity of humanity—I mean, I think it's inbred in human beings to want to believe that. To me, I think it's an idea I'd like to sweep away. Now, I might change my mind, I don't know, but right now, I don't have a lot of use for the idea.

MOTHER—I think we're learning things from each other!

Here's something else I wanted to say. There's this thing about the Rapture. I guess I'm terrible that I don't believe that Jesus is coming to take all the Christians and leave everyone else here on earth. I don't dare say that, so I keep my mouth shut. But the charismatics I've met—that's what they believe—and I can't see it. It's all based on the statement that Paul says, what he was inspired by. The disciples believed that Jesus was coming in their lifetimes. But it didn't happen. People all down the ages have believed that. I heard this from the time I was a little girl. But now I think that everyone will be taken care of—no matter what lies ahead for us. And I don't believe that I'm going up to heaven and everyone else who isn't a Christian will be left behind.

NANCY—Dad certainly believed it! That's the last thing I remember he told me a few days before he died. It was our last conversation. He had been feeling fine, even drove me out to have lunch at a local restaurant that day. When we returned, we sat down on the patio, and he continued talking about the Rapture. He'd been spouting those ideas to me for years, but that day he made everything concrete. He said, "I'm going tell you what's going to happen—it's going to happen soon. Your mother and I are going to be taken up in this golden chariot and ride across the sky into heaven—and I want to be sure that you take care of the house because vandals will get it." I think he had a premonition of his coming death—I really do.

MOTHER—I wonder if he believed all these things or whether he thought he *ought* to believe some of what was preached. I suspect that he didn't believe all of it. I doubt that he took the Rapture all that seriously because we would joke about it. If I couldn't find him around the house, I would go outside to find him puttering in the yard—I would say, "I thought you'd been Raptured!" And he would grin and laugh.

NANCY—Oh, I don't know. I think he tried to make up for his neglect of me by taking me out to lunch occasionally, and during those times he went through his litany of beliefs—they were just as crazy as the ones I remember from my teen-age years, but even more extreme—and one of them was that he was going to go up to heaven in that chariot. Of course, he never asked what I thought or believed—or whether I agreed with him! I think he naturally assumed that he was right and that people would fall in line with his thinking.

MOTHER—Now, about heaven and hell—I think those are states of consciousness. To me, hell would be the absence of being with God. Heaven would be the opposite. *If* there is an afterlife—and I'm really not convinced one way or other—whatever was good here on earth will prevail. Those are the ones who will be able to spend their time in God's presence. Those who didn't care about being good, I don't think they are going to be put into a fiery furnace. I can't believe in any kind of God that would create you only to put you into that state forever because you didn't believe a certain thing.

I don't know if my beliefs are right, but I think that those that have not expressed a desire to be good or that they don't want to be with God will be blotted out, period. That's enough hell, not to be with the state of things that are good—I don't think they are going to be punished! I might be irreligious, but that's what I think!

(In these last revelations, Mother became passionate. Her voice, while grainy with age, carried a resonance with much strong feeling. It was contrary to the controlled and quiet way expressed in the earlier interviews.)

NANCY—Now that's really interesting. I was thinking as you talked about the conversation we had—I don't think I recorded that on tape—about near-death experiences that lead us to think that there may be a consciousness beyond life and a connection with people they have known. But we don't know, of course, and some brain researchers say it's the chemicals that occur in the brain as it is dying. And nobody can tell us anything beyond what stories we hear from these people who have been brought back from nearly losing their lives.

But your comment that you couldn't believe that a God would create some kind of everlasting hell—that's exactly what some of the folks were saying when you were a little girl, but where you lived, you didn't get that message. There was a divergence in the evangelical movement—several groups. I know that the Universalists split off from other denominations like the Methodists and were active in the rural parts of the country. It's too bad that you didn't get their brand of religion. They couldn't believe in a God that would condemn different believers or non-believers to some kind of eternal damnation.

MOTHER—So that's why the Universalists separated? Because they couldn't believe in a literal heaven or hell?

NANCY—Or in a vengeful God. They departed from the Calvinist idea that certain people were predestined to be saved.

The Universalists thought that God was good and loved the whole universe. And that God was too loving and powerful not to include all peoples in the idea of being "saved." It was not too difficult to take the next step and acknowledge that there are profound insights in other cultures and Eastern religions as well as Christianity. And these ideas are often expounded upon by charismatic leaders, much as Jesus spoke to the people in his time of history. But their teachings would communicate to the specific culture out of which they arose. Before the Hebrews unified themselves, they engaged in pagan practices—that's what Old Testament prophets and leaders railed against.

MOTHER—It's been a long way and a long time, but I've come to think the way you describe—I didn't know about the Universalists, but we've come to the same conclusions.

NANCY—Until this conversation, I had no idea—I made assumptions about what you believed. You certainly surprised me, proved me wrong. I guess I have to thank you for keeping me humble.

(Right at this point, my mother spoke the words that will be forever emblazoned on my brain).

MOTHER—I firmly believe that all of us have been on a spiritual quest—and that none of us are at the end of this quest. That's what limits people. You have to know what you believe now, but you might have different insights later.

NANCY—Absolutely, and I would add that I feel that we are finite compared to the complexity of the universe—which is truly awesome and mysterious, and we will only glimpse a tiny fraction of what that great mystery is. At this point, some scientists are saying we may not be able to get back to what caused the Big Bang in the first place. Other scientists feel that we will discover someday what made life. What we do know is that certain chemicals came together, and they understand that. But they can't seem to tell us what preceded the bang—

what was the "nothing" that somehow became "something"? Scientists in the future may provide answers as to how and why exactly we came into being. Or we may never know, no matter how powerful our telescopes or how fast our computers are in crunching the numbers and giving answers to mathematical formulas—of course, that could change in the future—but right now there's a certain point beyond which the answers deal with tiny probabilities not final answers.

MOTHER—That idea is beautifully expressed in the Ninetieth Psalm. "Lord, you have been our dwelling place throughout all generations. Before the mountains were born or you brought forth the earth and the world, from everlasting to everlasting you are God."[13]

NANCY—That is truly awesome—a really profound thought. It's been enormously interesting to me as you traced your life and your conversion experiences—how you changed and why you changed and how you suffered and how you acted on it.

MOTHER—Yes, it's been kind of nice—

&⋄&

I thanked my mother for her candid conversation. I told her that I felt honored and humbled to be one of few confidantes in her life. I did not know that this was to be our last recorded interview. But something about those words—"it's been kind of nice"— communicated a sense of closure. I walked out of her house to my car, using my pocket flashlight to overcome the darkness. I drove west toward the home of my hosts, away from the mountains, away from city lights toward the valley near the river.

---

13   This wording of the Ninetieth Psalm is found in the *New International Version of The Bible*.

Afterword

Two months after these last three taped interviews, my mother fell and broke her arm. She became unable to care for herself, at which point I moved her to Colorado, where I now made my home. I located a comfortable board and care home near where we lived, and she stayed there for the next nine years. But the time came when the caring and compassionate caregivers in this facility could no longer handle her needs, and she spent the last three months of her life in a round-the-clock nursing home.

Only after her death did I realize that I had heard the amazing story of a quiet, ordinary woman, who had overcome difficulties, bitterness and blunders without religious counselors, psychotherapists, self-help books, confidantes, or support groups. She had endured the targeted sarcasm of an overbearing father, suffered the family shame of a mentally disturbed mother and lost a beloved sister to suicide. And at times, her being shook with fear for her soul.

Poetry moved her and helped bring her out of the darkness. A meaningful career path strengthened her. Love and friendship found her, and forgiveness cleansed her. She simply lived her life thrusting her way toward wholeness and health without much outside help. She did not seek to embark upon a spiritual quest. Instead, the process came to her, and in doing so, served up a dish of authenticity to flavor the journey.

These last tapes were as revelatory as the first shocking tales of my grandmother's attempted suicide and Emma's successful one. But my response this time was not that of shock and horror. Instead, her words pleasantly surprised me. I had not given credit to my mother's superior independence of mind. I was amazed that she could keep her own counsel, feeling bonded to her church community because of its outreach of love and support, yet differing widely from its theological belief system, the specifics of which she kept to herself. And she did it all with confidence and serenity, secure and supported in her knowledge of a presence within—a personal relationship with a loving and caring God.

For me, these last conversations were the source of enlightenment about where I had fallen short. I had assumed that my mother's habits and beliefs were static and inflexible, as I remembered them in childhood. I was trapped in my own prejudice, certain that I, but surely not my parent, would ever change. How arrogant was I to think this way! Although I could point to examples in her child rearing that led me to this conclusion, I simply could not ignore that she had upended all my prior impressions. In sharing her life with me, she had inspired me with words of hope, liberation and affirmation.

Chapter 16

Lessons from the Well: A Daughter's Redemption

Therefore with joy shall ye draw water out of the wells of salvation.

—Isaiah 12:3

So here is what I learned. Once upon time two women—my mother and I—embarked upon a journey. At the beginning, Mother was amazingly active at seventy-seven, while I was at the prime of my life in my middle thirties. I initiated the adventure so that I could learn about my mother's growing up and about her experiences before I ever entered her life. And I wanted to see if we could heal a rift in our relationship. The trip was long, sixteen years to be exact. At first I led the way, drawing out my mother's answers to my endless questions. She shared herself willingly, constantly surprising me with fresh doses of frankness and a sense of humor as she related the tales of her childhood and young adult life. Some of her memories told of pain. Some imparted recollections of simple pleasures. A few of the stories were about tragedies. Others were tales of triumphant achievements, told modestly in her unique, self-effacing way. Still others brought us smiles and laughter.

As the tales unfolded, I pondered the meaning of the journey for my own life in nighttime dreams and waking thoughts. Often these blurred together, confusing me as to their origin. I began to write down these fleeting impressions in my journal, trying to put them in some kind of order.

In one dream, a young girl approached a well. Pools of tears filled the girl's eyes. Dressed in a simple muslin frock with an apron, she moved toward the well, intending to plunge herself into its watery depths. On the side of the well was a sign, "The Well of Despair." But wait, a shimmering image began to take form from the watery depths of the well. Someone was calling, wailing from down inside the well. Was this visage the girl's mother? Or the girl herself, crying out and weeping for her mother? Who was in the well? Who was outside the well? The dream tumbled chaotically as different figures emerged. Into this dream came people from ancient times. Possibly I had been unconsciously thinking of Demeter weeping by the well for her daughter Persephone, snatched into the underworld by Hades. There was a nightmarish quality to this dream, enough to bring shudders upon my awakening.

In another dream, a relatively young woman stood at the same well. Instead of a flowered dress with an apron, she wore a nurse's uniform with a winged hat clipped to the sides of her head. This time, the sign read, "The Well of Self-Discovery." A woman approached cautiously, grabbed the bucket suspended by ropes, and lowered it into the water. She managed to wind up the rope and catch the bucket, which splashed water all over her uniform. She dipped in a ladle and sipped the cool water. Out of nowhere, a man came walking toward her. He was in contemporary clothing, and he wore a mask. Was this a bandit, come to harm her? The man asked her to give him a drink. She shrank from his approach as if she had some vague recollection of knowing this man and feeling that he was intruding on her space. With trepidation, she extended the ladle. As he drank, he looked directly at her, reached up to his face and removed his mask. He faced her, and she recognized him. He spoke, "You will know the truth, and the truth will make you free." This dream, I felt, had to do with confronting Jesus speaking a profound lesson in how to liberate ourselves from our worst misgivings.

I awakened, gripped by this dream. What "truth" must be faced, and what was the woman in the dream supposed to discover? Was the man in the dream suggesting that the truth of our real lives lies behind the masks we don, behind the fears we bury, behind the hurts we shelter? And to be free of these demons, we need to "unmask" our true selves? This dream was not as disturbing as the earlier one. The feeling upon waking was one of enlightenment, as if an "aha" moment has occurred.

As my mother and I neared the end of our conversation time together, I had yet a third "well" dream. In this one, an older woman with gray hair and hazel eyes shuffled along, steadying herself with a cane, moving ponderously toward a stone well. Sprouting at its base was a scraggly lilac bush holding but a few last blooms of the season. When she reached the well, a fresh bucket of water already was drawn up for her. Milling around was a huge throng of people beckoning to the woman, possibly those whose lives had intertwined with hers over the years. Others seemed to be ancient souls, some who have really lived, some only known in myth or stories or poetry. They were gently swaying as if they were one person. And another sign appeared, this time reading "The Well of Harmony." Into the bucket the old woman dipped her cup and drank deeply. Before turning to leave the well, she stooped down to pluck a lilac from the withered bush. "See?" she said, turning toward the group of people. "It's from the past, it's from now, it will be there in the future." Once again she spoke, saying something about the world being imperfect but that she wanted to enjoy the intense beauty of it all while she could. Another fragment intruded. The aging woman frowned as if she had forgotten to say something important, something special. The dream character said, "Ah, it is forgiveness. Don't forget that, it will make your life whole." The last part I recall is of swaying souls gathering around the woman, smiling at her, soothing her, and leading her off. I sensed that she was surrounded by a community of love.

Once again, I tried to interpret how this dream had affected me. It felt mournful but also deeply peaceful, as if some kind of balance had been achieved. And it seemed to be speaking to the acceptance of reality, the dealing with loss, but holding fast the loveliness that pervades everywhere, all around us. As I wrote my notes, I also tucked their lessons away in my heart.

What were the lessons?

First and foremost, I realized that my mother was not the person I felt I knew in childhood. The pilgrimage together had led me to a new view of my mother, as if I now "saw" with crisper lenses. What if I had clung to the original stereotype?

Oh, how different would be my knowledge of both my mother's life and my own, and how much joy and sharing and laughter and tears we would have missed had we not embarked upon this adventure!

Secondly, the "well dreams" led me to think about the importance of digging deep into the wellspring within myself, to face my fears and destroy my own demons. I speculated that these were not exclusive to those who have suffered deprivation in the manner of her mother. No, they lay everywhere in all of us, as did the memories of the vicissitudes—often painful—of my mother's life. But somewhere within is the capacity to reach down and draw up healing waters. The well could be a place for seeking strength and granting grace. Even so, I saw that the well within could be a temptress, where we could go to drown our despair. Choices present themselves: plunging into the darkness of the well, or drawing up the bucket into the light and drinking from those life-giving waters. Remembering my mother's conversion experiences, I had my own "aha moment": In tapping my inner resources lay the possibility of salvation.

Another lesson lay in the powerful story of my mother's encounter with the benefits of forgiveness. Were there any in my life I yet needed to forgive? I had to admit that denial was easy and admission was difficult. But I saw that I, too, would need to experience moments of forgiveness over and over as a practiced way of living my life. With my mother's story forever playing out in my brain, I knew that my own efforts would occasionally backslide. Aiming for perfection but finding it elusive, my mother did detriment to her soul. This insight led her into more charitable ways of living her life. Thus I learned, paradoxically, that I must accept that life would forever be imperfect. The payoff lay in Mother's lesson: From forgiveness can arise a peaceful harmony that illuminates all potential in life.

A final lesson had to do with the notion of time passing. I faced that I could not stop my own progression into old age. When the recordings began, I had a young child. But the child grew up, married and established her own household. A few years after the last tape was made, my own daughter became a mother herself, making me a grandmother of two. Armed with these memories, I need not mourn the passing of my youth and young adult life but rather embrace the possibilities of each moment left to me. I could resist the inevitable marching of time or immerse myself in my own creative work. I could withdraw or engage in satisfying relationships with family and friends. I could complain or go forth living and loving with joy. Time would change all things around me except for one thing –I would forever cherish the woman who gave me birth. The two of us would be linked, along with all other mothers and grandmothers before us, in my survivors' memory through some kind of cosmic consciousness.

The journey began with my eliciting stories from my mother, who graciously agreed to trudge along the road of recollection. As our trek through the past neared its end, she was very old but still mentally keen. But now she was the leader. Taking me by the hand, she became my guide, managing to smash all of my preconceptions about her. We had come full circle, each through our own separate redemptive journeys. In our last moments together, we came to the end of the quest, hand in hand, like two streams now merged into one rushing river, tumbling through canyons, cutting and deepening the earth. Now it was time for me to tell this remarkable story and continue my own journey, carrying a mythical water jug of wisdom into which my mother had poured sacred waters.

Epilogue

November 2003

Early November is a perfect season to visit New Mexico. This is the time of year for scents of piñon smoke so pungent it reminds me of my childhood. Sunny days, cool nights, golden cottonwoods. These are the memories stashed away in my brain and my heart.

This is the best time to see the Sandhill Cranes in their yearly migration to Bosque del Apache, a national wildlife refuge 100 miles south of Albuquerque. In the morning, I arise early to take a walk on the acequia, a canal that carries the river water to distant fields. I have missed these yearly visits of the cranes. They fill the sky with their haunting cries, sustained throbs like wavering violin strings. And I am missing my mother, too, for she has been gone now for exactly one year.

The cottonwoods along the ditch shimmer as the sunlight yawns and stretches to greet a new fall day. As I squint up at the sky past the shafts of sunlight, I catch the first calls of the cranes. From the distance, I hear the beginning of a thrum, a monotonous tone that rises into a crescendo of long wails as the flock passes over. They move as one great gray mass soaring with sheer elegance, precisely in formation, flapping those incredible six-foot wings.

And then I see them—first one white Whooping Crane, then another following close by. They are a bit larger than the Sandhills. Together, they punch a hole in the dark pencil sketch swarming above. They glide, flashing white against the brilliant blue of a New Mexico sky. Seeing them is special because the Whoopers are endangered. I follow the flight with my head tilted upward, my neck moving in an arc along with the cranes. The noise above my head nearly splits my ears for a few seconds. Directly overhead, with each glint of sun on their underbellies, I catch only ochre, not gray. Their magnificent wings stir the air and rustle the cottonwood leaves as they head toward their refuge, carrying away their wails of woe. Two white flashes appear amongst a streaking mass of gray.

I plant my feet on the sandy bank of the acequia and peer up through the golden leaves of the cottonwood trees. Casting my eyes downward, I see muddy water flowing past, a rippling brown ribbon tying together earth and sky. I think of some of our mother-daughter conversations with the tape recorder humming, capturing stories that broke through the distance we had placed between us: the afternoon when the sea breezes blew into our lives the spirits of the past, the evening when we watched the sunset reflected on the mighty mountains and spoke of loss and forgiveness, and the time when we disclosed our innermost spiritual beliefs to each other. The finality of all that has happened sweeps over me. There will be no more meetings, except in memory, except in words, except in tears.

But right now, for a few minutes on a fall morning, I get to watch the cranes soaring overhead. The cranes will fly year after year, but never again will my mother join me in person for our pilgrimage. Still, I am witness to a rare sight—two birds, slightly different from the rest, fly in formation with a huge flock, all in beautiful symmetry and harmony. And I feel that a miracle has passed my way.

Appendix: Some Writings

From Emma's "Bits and Pieces"

*[My mother found "The Fool's Prayer," by Edward Rowland Sill
(1841-1887) in Emma's folder entitled "Bits and Pieces." Below
are the parts of the poem my mother refers to as showing her how
depressed Emma was.]*

The royal feast was done; the King
Sought some new sport to banish care,
And to his jester cried: "Sir Fool,
Kneel now, and make for us a prayer!"

The jester doffed his cap and bells,
And stood the mocking court before;
He could not see the bitter smile
Behind the painted grin he wore.

He bowed his head, and bent his knee
Upon the Monarch's silken stool;
His pleading voice arose: "O Lord,
Be merciful to me, a fool!"

These clumsy feet, still in the mire
Go crushing blossoms without end;
These hard, well-meaning hands we thrust
Among the heart-strings of a friend.

The ill-timed truth we might have kept—
Who knows how sharp it pierced and stung?
The word we had not sense to say –
Who knows how grandly it had rung!

Nancy Key Roeder

Two Poems by Laura Catherine Delaney Johnson

Seeking[14]

If I could catch one perfect, fluttering thing
Within my net of words, or if fate chose
My brain to yield from out the hidden spring
Of consciousness the watering for one rose
Of finished loveliness; or when I've won
From out that soil one perfect gem of thought,
And see its colors flashing in the sun,
And feel sweet ecstasy in what I've wrought;
Still may I have no peace until I find
That finite hearts are much too faint and small,
And much too narrow is the finite mind
To catch and hold eternity in thrall;
That beauty follows after, is not caught:
The whole pursued me while the part I sought.

—1932

---

14   This poem of my mother's was published under her real name in *Sunset Magazine* in 1935.

Plagiarism

A plagiarist am I: The thoughts that I
Call mine are only grains of bright gold dust
Dropped from the cosmic polishing wheel which turns
Upon the axis of infinity –
Perpetually whirling, and on which is burnished
Little by little, one facet at a time
The Thing we call Perfection, Excellence,
Truth, Beauty, and a thousand other names.

And all the pictures I absurdly thought
Had been brought forth from my own pot of paint
Were made the First Artist's brush
Upon a cloud or on an autumn hill,
Or on a desert canvas, lighted by
His own white candle, and all set around
By an unpolished frame of uncut gems—
A million-pieced mosaic. Or somewhere
Upon a darkened background he has thrown
A mighty storm in heedless grandeur riding,
With sureness filling laws immutable.

Or penciled on a leaden winter sky
Great, lovely trees, with their unblushing forms
In their distorted shapeliness unveiled.
And on a lighter canvas He has splashed

A bed of homely zinnias, showing forth
With candor all their elemental colorings.

The happy songs which sometimes seem to flow
From out my heart and from my finger tips
Were whispered first by Him to thrush and lark
And cardinal, and all their feathered kind.

And to the mountain streams He told the secret
Of all the melodies that ever were
Or ever can be. I have taken themes
From sibilant sign of pine trees in the wind
Or from the syncopated dropping sound
Of chestnuts from the soft brown lips
That sever, giving them nativity.

So, I'm a plagiarist: my work not to create
But to discover all the sparks of excellence
That fly from every facet of embodied Beauty
Before they twinkle out, and polish them
Devotedly, and call forth every gleam
Of luster that is comprehended in
Each tiny grain; to have but eyes to see
The paintings covering every inch of wall
Of this great room—this gallery of art,
And studiously reproduce them on
A smaller scale; to have but ears to hear
The faint sweet whispering of each speaking pipe
Of that cathedral organ played upon
By music's perfect Head. And then I'll feel
My brain and heart and fingers kissed
With sweet forgiveness, that I am a plagiarist.

—1934

Discussion Questions

1. In this book, the story emerges through tape recorded interviews between the author and her mother. If you taped your parents' stories, how do you think they would respond? Would they be candid or restrained? Do you believe they would find it easy to share with other family members the difficult times from their lives?

2. The author begins the conversations with her mother as a way to establish better communication. What would be your expectations if you tried to heal a rift with one or both of your parents? What initial steps could you take that might be beneficial?

3. The Author's Note (p. 9) refers to the fallibility of memory, especially "emotional memory." What does "emotional memory" mean to you? Can it color recollections of what really happened in the past? Is there a difference between completely accurate detail of past events and feelings that linger for a lifetime? Which truths are more valid?

4. A major thread is how the relationship between mother and daughter changes over time. What lessons does the author learn about relating to her mother? Have you experienced changes in the way you view your parents? If so, what changes?

5. The author's in-depth encounter with her mother could apply equally to one's father. If you explored your relationship with your mother or father, do you feel you could benefit from understanding their experiences? Even if your mother or father is no longer living, could you still learn something valuable by contemplating the past?

6. The first section of the book, "Revelation," taps the author's mother's memories of early childhood in rural America. Do you believe in the "good old days"? Did they exist, and if so, what characterized them? How difficult or easy is it to empathize with the life of someone who lived three generations ago? What has changed, and what has stayed the same?

7. The author's mother reveals that she strove to fit into the family, but often felt alternating instances of acceptance and rejection. At various times she refers to herself as "weird," "odd," or "the one who left." What do you think makes her feel this way? Do you know

people who have struggled to be themselves while still trying to be part of their families or social groups in general? How do they achieve mastery of this difficult task?

8. The author mentions in Chapter 16 (p. 223) that the journey with her mother caused her to re-evaluate assumptions and preconceptions. What assumptions have you drawn from relationships with your parents that may be unwarranted? What could you do or have you done to correct those assumptions?

9. The author's mother reports how fear-based religion affected her happiness in growing up. She says that she probably absorbed these religious messages more deeply and more negatively than did her siblings. In what ways do some people internalize religion negatively while others experience more positive reactions to identical exposure?

10. Another part of the story deals with psychological ruptures experienced by several family members. (Chapter 7, p. 113, "… when you lose but don't lose your mother.") What were some of the lingering effects on the author's mother? What decisions did she make to compensate for and work through the hardships of her past? What have you done in your life to overcome a bad deal of the cards?

11. The story unfolds with the telling of tragic events that affected the family deeply. Can you ever know another person well enough to make a valid judgment about his or her choice of suicide as a response to life circumstances? When tragedy strikes a family, what coping mechanisms are employed to survive?

12. The author's mother speaks in Chapter 13 of the liberating power of forgiveness. Are there people that you have forgiven or need to forgive? What benefit do you see in letting go of past hurts?

13. The "well" figures in the story as both a real place and a symbolic one. In Chapter 16 (p. 222), the author imagines it as an emotional space to drown sorrows or, conversely, to find inner strength. What have you discovered in your own "well" that might benefit your life?

About the Author

Nancy Key Roeder is a retired high school English teacher. She grew up in New Mexico, beginning her work career as a reporter and feature writer for *The Albuquerque Tribune*. Subsequently, she published numerous free-lance articles and essays in local and regional newspapers and nationally distributed magazines. She holds a B.A. in English from San Francisco State University and a Master of Social Science degree from the University of Colorado at Denver. She lives in Denver, Colorado and this is her first book.

www.ingramcontent.com/pod-product-compliance
Lightning Source LLC
Chambersburg PA
CBHW031121020426
42333CB00012B/177